Breaking The Cycle Of Trauma

Through A Daughter's Eyes

Susan Laurie Magestro

Copyright © 2024 Susan Laurie Magestro

All rights reserved. This book may not be reproduced in whole or in part without the written consent of the author.

This Publication is sold as is without warranty. The author will not be held liable for damages arising from this publication or its contents.

The companies mentioned in this publication are for identification only.

ISBN: 978-1-7372512-4-8
Cover and book design: Bill Garret

Published by:
Magestro & Associates, LLC
phone: (907) 529-7151
e-mail: sulamaestra@gmail.com
www.susanmagestro.com

Printed in the United States of America.

Dedication

There are three things we want to know when we think about death:

*Our life had purpose; we made a difference or impact on the lives of others
*We loved and knew we were loved
*We will be remembered
It's that simple!

Dedicated to my mother- Always Loved

Table of Contents

Prologue 1

Chapter One: Mirror, Mirror on The Wall 5

Chapter Two: In My Early Years 9

Chapter Three: Our Life, Our Normal 15

Chapter Four: Sweet Sixteen, Not So Sweet 25

Chapter Five: Virginity Confirmed 31

Chapter Six: Validation of A Rape 37

Chapter Seven: To Escort or Not to Escort 45

Chapter Eight: The Calm Before the Storm 49

Chapter Nine: The Wedding That Throws a Punch 55

Chapter Ten: Happy New Baby! Don't Call Me Again! 63

Chapter Eleven: Moving Far Away 69

Chapter Twelve: The Affair That Never Happened 79

Chapter Thirteen: The Beginning of The End 81

Chapter Fourteen: Getting the Attention of Others 91

Chapter Fifteen: Selling the Family Home 95

Chapter Sixteen: A Final Image 103

Chapter Seventeen: Finally At Peace 111

Chapter Eighteen: Family Ever After 119

Epilogue 123

Stages of Borderline Personality Disorder 127

Characteristics of a Borderline Personality Disorder 133

How I Broke the Cycles of Trauma 134

What is Borderline Personality Disorder? 137

Photographs 139

About Author 155

Prologue

The Borderline parent cannot love their child the way other parents can. They justify their own inability to love the child by blaming the child. The parent sees their child's milestones as alienation and as a personal attack that the child does not want to be near their parent any longer.

These parents do not have an understanding of the normal stages of child development. Instead, they feel threatened by their child's independence, so they attempt to sabotage every milestone their child achieves. They do this because they believe that if they make the child feel no one will ever want them, the child will stay with them forever. In their core, the borderline parent fears abandonment, yet they present as quite the opposite.

The borderline wife loves her spouse and children as much as she is capable of. Yet, she disregards all boundaries and keeps a mental list of all their vulnerabilities, stripping them of the dignities they deserve. Most husbands divorce their borderline wives, but a few will remain in the marriage. Over time, those that stay become convinced that no one wants to be around them and they eventually believe they are not worthy as husbands. It is guesstimated that a majority of borderlines are women.

Recognizing a borderline personality occurs as a slow process. It presents as psychotic rages, oftentimes leaving the targeted spouse or child apologizing for everything. Unfortunately, in time, the husband and children become grateful to this woman for loving them, believing no one else ever will. The culmination of this emotional roller coaster ride leaves them without a sense of self. Many of their children leave home as soon as they can without ever knowing or understanding the trauma they have lived in, thus not working through the trauma until later in life, if at all.

For many, you will read this story and see this world through the eyes of an observer. You will gain new insight into the trauma and lives of these children.

The home of a borderline is one of constant inconsistencies. Family members will experience the borderline raging one moment, loving the next, followed by insulting and humiliating comments and actions. There is a deep disrespect for the dignity and boundaries for those who become the targets of a borderline.

After each of these psychotic episodes, as they are called by professionals, the borderline parent denies that the events ever happened. They refuse to take responsibility for anything they said or did. This makes living with a borderline even more confusing and unsettling for their family members.

Be it a mundane or stressful event, anything can trigger their symptoms, often unexpectedly, as their anger is based on their interpretation or perception of situations. Sometimes, a borderline sees anger in the faces of someone who is emotionally neutral. The threats they continue to feel are often based on a lack of reality. Yet to them, they perceive the threats as justified.

For many more, my story will provide answers to questions about your own childhood, ones you have held inside for many years. For some readers, you will want to reach out after finishing this book and share your revelations. I hope that you do reach out.

Looking back, I wish I would have known about borderline personality disorder. It would have made my early years so much more bearable. But most of all, it would have allowed me to be more patient and understanding of my mother, instead of shell shocked and confused. I would have handled so many situations with more thoughtfulness. Frequently, I felt I needed to run away from her. There were long spans of time when we did not speak. I was always shocked by the outrageous things she would say and took them to heart. Knowing about my mother's personality disorder would have prevented so much frustration on my part. I never completely cut the parent-child bond, but I was protective of my children for fear she would be the same with them. Like all borderlines, she had her targets. If you were one of those targets, God help you. If you were not, she was absolutely delightful and everyone loved her.

I was with my mother during her last days. Her death impacted her family in a way no one could have predicted. It is a story that I feel in my soul every time I think of her and my father. My family history compels me to share my story, not just as a criminologist, but also as a daughter.

It is my hope that however you relate to my story, it will assist you to navigate your own personal and professional journey to change the trajectory of the lives of the children, families, and clients who live with borderlines. For some, like me, this will give you the understanding to make changes and break the cycle of generational trauma. However, I've discovered that as hard as I try, I have restricted memories and cannot remember more specific examples than what is included in this book. I am able to accept these limitations and move forward without the desire to unlock anything more in this area of my life.

I owe my career as an international criminologist to my mother. It is not the books I have read or my graduate and professional degrees that make me who I am professionally. It is my mother who taught me to be the professional I have become over the last thirty years. It is my mother who taught me first- hand about chronic, complex, and generational trauma. In the end, it was looking at my mother through my father's loving eyes that allowed me to process forgiveness in time and move forward in my own life; breaking the cycle of trauma.

Chapter One:

Mirror, Mirror on The Wall

My mother was beautiful. Throughout my childhood, I was constantly told how beautiful she was. There was beauty as she looked into the mirror, but I often wonder if she saw beauty looking back. Deep down, I thought she was evil and ugly. I desperately wanted to think she was beautiful as well, but I never did. I felt badly about that and questioned if something must be wrong with me.

I have stayed close with many of the families in the town where I grew up. All but one were unaware of mother's behaviors towards me and my dad. One of the teenage boys who is now an older man, recently shared with me that many of the neighborhood boys considered my mother a MILF. He asked if I knew what that was. With a sick feeling in my stomach, I told him I did.

Mother could dress with a sense of style and flare few could match. She portrayed confidence and poise. Mother was dramatic in her presentation, knowing exactly how to perfect her makeup and accessorize with every outfit, with magnificent jewelry and sometimes hats. She posed for pictures like she was a model. Sometimes the camera would capture her flirty side. Other times her appearance varied which made it hard to recognize her moods. It was only as she aged that the camera picked up her hard edge. It was fascinating to me that the two times she sat with me for painted portraits, both artists painted her exactly as I knew her to be (cold and disconnected).

She was a stay at home mother, but she didn't like it much. She referred to me as her 'damn kid'. I kept trying to be good, hoping she would stop thinking of me that way, but it never changed no matter what I did.

As a child, I grew up in a constant state of fear and confusion. Deep down I believed there was something very wrong with me. Mother insisted no man would ever want to marry me and I believed her. "I feel bad for the man that marries you," she would say more times than I can count.

Being raised by a borderline mother turned out to be a gift of sorts. I became a master at watching for mother's shark eyes and listening to her voice. Listening to the lilt in her voice gave me a clue as to what kind of a day we were going to have. This would become the base for the professional tools that I use today. It made me familiar with and not uncomfortable in the world of anger and violence.

This life with my mother became my normal. When I began my career, working with children who live with trauma and violence, I was in my comfort zone. Mother gave me the gift of a hyper-vigilant sensitivity with a grounded sense of calm that has led me throughout my career. She taught me to read shark eyes, mean eyes, sad eyes, and calm eyes. Children of borderlines can identify each other without saying a word. These children, youth or adults, can look into my eyes and see the safety they feel they lack in their own lives. This is one of the gifts mother inadvertently gave to me, to help those, some of who are just like me.

There are more than five million parents like mine, from Stages One to Four, displaying behaviors that vary in intensity. Many of these parents are not as violent and perverse as mine. It is not only the children of borderlines who struggle; their spouses often live a tortuous life as well, until they just can't take it anymore. Usually they divorce; my father was one of the few exceptions.

Dad stayed married to mother for fifty-five years, but it cost him dearly. For the last twenty-five years of their marriage, he stopped talking, responding with an occasional yes, or grunts. He shut down and withdrew. It was only upon her death that he started talking again. Dad started to enjoy his life. He even had two girlfriends. What a gift to be able to hear his kind and gentle voice once again. I cherished every moment of it.

At the time my mother died, I thought her death was one of the most freeing moments of my life. It felt like a weight had been lifted from my shoulders. Conversely, there were also times when I would become deeply sad, sad at the finality that I would never foster a normal relationship with my mother. At the end, as more psychiatrists were called upon to address her increasing violence, I was able to see her through a different set of eyes; those of a scared animal. And it was the fear in her eyes that compelled me to stand by a woman who was so tortured. I prayed every moment that God would finally give this tortured woman some peace.

I will always remember the final two conversations I had with my mother. She smiled and told me what a beautiful woman I was and without missing a beat added that she still thought I was a bitch. The last time I saw her, I had all of her grandchildren, sons-in-law, and great grandchildren sitting in a circle around her. There were ten of us and one of the granddaughters was about to deliver another baby. We brought mother mint chocolate chip ice cream, her favorite, and shared one of her favorite past times, eating ice cream. With tears in her eyes, she looked at me and said, "You always said you were going to have a big family and you did." My heart ached as we all wanted so desperately to love her, hear her infectious laugh, and listen to her sing. Instead we had to do this from afar. I like to think she is a peaceful and joyous angel laughing and singing as she watches us from above. That is the beautiful picture I hold moving forward.

Chapter Two:

In My Early Years

I always thought my father was a wonderful man. I felt like the luckiest child in the world to have a father so handsome, so strong, and so charismatic. He was a passionate man filled with never ending barrels of love. His love was far reaching for his wife, his child, his grandchildren, his mother, his sister and brother, his nieces, and nephews. These were the people in his life, his people. They made him smile from ear to ear. Their joys were his joys. He was a man who made you feel like you were the most wonderful, special person in the world.

He would sing when he drove, sometimes off key. He spoke with conviction at our black and white television reacting to the news coverage of the changing times. He would shake his head and tell us he couldn't acclimate to the changing world.

Dad never spoke badly about those he loved, never. He taught us, "If you can't say something nice, don't say anything at all." He seemed to live a happy life. I can only think of two times I ever saw my father become angry. I believe he loved my mother so completely, he pushed aside the critical words she spoke to him. He lived that motto until he died. There was enough fun with mother that the positive seemed to outweigh the nastiness. They had date night every Saturday night and mother would dress up. Every Wednesday night they took classes together; dancing on skates, Latin dancing classes, refinishing furniture. I think as a child I thought they were happy and maybe they were. When I was about eight years old, I remember that some days when I came home from school, mother would be smiling. She would share that dad came home for lunch and they had sex. It was great, she would add. It was a love I did not understand.

Dad was gone a lot, working all day and into the night. He worked Saturdays as well. He wasn't home a lot. I loved his voice as it was so soothing and kind, until he spoke no more. I heard him speak for the last time when he was fifty-three years old. Then he ceased speaking. He did not speak again until his wife, my mother, was dying, over twenty- five years later.

Dad had lost his own father at the young age of thirteen. Grandpa Sam, died suddenly of a heart attack. A year later, dad's older sister, Sarah, died shortly after childbirth. Dad had walked into Sarah's hospital room excited to congratulate her on the birth of her new baby son, but the bed was empty. Both she and the baby had died and he didn't know. He experienced death firsthand, losing his father, his sister, and nephew, all within one year.

His mother, my Grandma Jenny, as sole support of her family, went to work as an intensive care baby nurse when dad was entering his teen years. This required her to be away from home for weeks at a time. Dad cared for himself or spent time with his older sister, Dottie. Dottie always made him feel welcome and he adored his only remaining sister, but it wasn't the same. She had four children of her own, and he was not one of them. I believe he was viewed and felt like an outsider.

Dad met mother at a beach and married her less than a year later. He was smitten with mother, her beauty, her confidence, and laughter. Mother was eager to move out of her father's house and dad was lonely.

They had a small wedding ceremony and started their lives living in a basement apartment in the city. I believe they were very happy during this time. Dad finally had the family he always wanted and mother had a house to call their own.

I was born about a year and a half into their marriage. Mother was excited to have a daughter, a best friend, she told everyone. Mother had no experience being around babies and young children. The dream of having a daughter to do things with and confide in made her life complete.

I was a happy baby for the first few months. Something happened to me after that. I was losing weight rapidly. Mother claimed I was unable to keep down the bottles of formula she gave me. My pediatrician became increasingly more concerned as my weight by six months of age plummeted.

I was brought to New York Children's Hospital at six months old. Mother said I was admitted for not being able to keep anything down because I looked so thin. I later learned that in reality, I was a failure to thrive baby who was rapidly losing weight. Doctors admitted me for almost a month, observing me and running many tests.

Mother insisted my doctors do exploratory surgery. They would not. Their compromise was a series of x-rays, exposing me to unnecessary radiation. My doctors never found a reason for my failure to thrive. There weren't any blockages, nor was there anything physical to explain what they were seeing. All the doctors and nurses observed was a fussy baby, not soothed by a beautiful, well dressed, young mother. Their notes did not indicate anything out of the ordinary. Nothing stood out to them. At least nothing she allowed them to see.

Towards the end of my stay in the hospital, I started to gain weight and was discharged. Discharge instructions included frequent follow up visits with my pediatrician and were scheduled by hospital staff. To this day, I wonder if they considered or discussed that what they were looking at was a Munchausen Syndrome by Proxy, a co-morbidity of what was to come later.

Dad worked longer hours to pay the hospital bills. The day after I was brought home, mother called friends and family to let them know she had saved my life. She had alleged that the medication the hospital sent home for me was actually the medication for an adult male with a heart condition. She claims I was napping during the time I was due for the first dose of the medicine. She never gave me the dose that "surely would have killed me." She claimed by allowing me to sleep through this "error by the hospital," she saved my life. Mother claims she threw the medication down the toilet before dad got home that night.

Mother loved to retell that story. "I let her live, I mean sleep," she would say. To this day, I wonder if there really was a medication or this was one of the stories which would become indicative of mother's displaying symptoms of Munchausen Syndrome. I never learned the answer to this.

After this alleged incident, it seemed only natural Grandma Jenny would move in with us. She offered to help mother with the stresses of handling such a sick baby. Grandma was a respected and well sought after baby nurse, but her proposal was not well received or appreciated by my mother.

Jenny was strong, confident, and very strict. She wore heavy shoes. Her steps could be heard a mile away. Jenny had strawberry blonde hair. Even though she was petite, she came across like a giant to all her grandchildren.

Grandma didn't live with us for long, only a few weeks. I'm told she couldn't live with mother's frequent rages, struggling to just stand by and listen to the continual verbal attacks. Mother experienced episodes where she loved you and hated you vehemently all within a few minutes, Dad would become sheepish responding to mother's flirtations followed by withdrawal after each episode of rage. We all grew used to mother's "I love you, I hate you" flipping but we never grew less wary from the exhaustion her ranting caused.

Grandma Jenny was worried about the emotional and physical safety for both her son and me, her granddaughter. She tried to talk to dad about her concerns, but he was unreachable. Besides him working long hours, dad was deeply in love with his wife and new baby. This was the family he had always wanted. Dad would tell me mother just had a temper and we needed to be careful not to upset her. I never knew what would upset her. I felt like I was walking on eggshells all of the time.

There are moments when I wonder what that must have been like for my grandmother. It must have been difficult for her to walk away. It is beyond my comprehension to understand how she coped with the realization that there was nothing she could do to protect her son or granddaughter from living in such a volatile situation. In those days, one kept their feelings to themselves, so I don't believe these concerns were voiced to the rest of the family at that time.

Dad was in love and didn't want to hear what his mother was saying. No one wanted to believe the evils of which my mother could be capable of.

I have only limited memories of my early years. My earliest memories begin at about age four with my maternal grandparents. I loved my Grandma Molly and Grandpa Ted, mother's parents. Grandma Molly was so petite, sweet, and demure. She was always a pleaser. Grandpa Ted was larger than life and quite the trickster. He would get me bundled up in my coat and hat to get ready to go to the park then motion me to walk in front of him out their apartment door. Then he'd close the door behind me and lock me out. That usually lasted until I broke down in tears. Then he'd scoop me up for a big hug and he would say teasingly, "I was only kidding Shoo -Shoo."

I had my own special drawer at their apartment. It was in the hutch in their dining room. Every time I came to visit them they had a new surprise in "my special drawer".

Grandpa died right before my fifth birthday and I remember Grandma Molly stayed with us for a while. I remember telling her, "Don't be sad grandma, we will take care of you."

I loved my Grandma Molly. She made the best hamburgers. I don't think it was the salt or the pepper that made them taste so yummy, but the love she put into them, gently flipping them a dozen times so they were cooked equally all around.

I was told that Grandma Molly and Grandpa Ted had a difficult and turbulent marriage. He was known to be an alcoholic and had a hair trigger temper. He was either working making money or dead broke. "Money just slipped through his hands," people used to say. Grandma Molly worked at Macy's in the Housewares Department. That was unusual in the 1950's when most women stayed home and raised the children. My grandmother had three living children and six back alley procedures on grandpa's insistence, claiming those children could not be afforded.

One day when grandma came home from working at Macy's, she found my grandpa lying on top of my mother. My mother told me this story and insisted that they had their clothes on. I learned this from mother when I was eight years old. I wasn't exactly sure what all of it meant, but I knew it wasn't a good thing. Grandma Molly told him he better never do that again or she was going to kill him. Mother told me it was difficult at her home after that because her father treated her differently. After sharing that story, when I was eight years old, my mother seldom spoke of my grandfather and we had no contact with his family.

I have often wondered if some of the experiences I encountered with mother were as a result of her claims of abuse by her father. I have often considered the trauma my mother must have lived with and asked myself if her flipping outbursts were as a result of her childhood (nurture) or was it genetic (nature). Did she walk on eggshells or live in fear as a child growing up?

Chapter Three:

Our Life, Our Normal

While most children can look at their mother with affection and feel warmth at the sight of her smile, I have memories of my mother pouring milk over my head at age eight. One day after school, she gave me a glass of milk and milk made me sick. I said I couldn't drink it because it hurt my belly and suddenly she grabbed the glass and poured it over my head. Then she made me go out and play without allowing me to wipe the milk away.

My rescue continued to be my neighbor, Angela. With a sad smile, she wiped my face, gave me a hug and a snack. She sat with me as I ate, asking me about my day. When I finished, she encouraged me to go play with the rest of the children playing kickball on our street. I felt secure with Angela. She used to tell me she needed to teach me how to make the best Italian food, so I could grow up and marry one of her sons. I always smiled when she said that, half hoping that would be true. I wanted her to be a part of my life forever.

After another hug, I ran out to play with the other children. I loved the families who lived on my street. Playing outside with the other children and visiting with their parents were some of the calmest parts of my day.

I started kindergarten three months before my fifth birthday. That was way too young. But mother told me she was anxious and ready to get me out of the house.

Frequently she told me she just didn't have patience for me, I drained her. Occasionally, she would end with I guess I'm not child person. I didn't understand what any of that meant.

It was a constant struggle to keep up with the other children at school both socially and academically, since I was always one of the youngest in my grade.

When I attended first and second grade, I became aware of two different parts to my day, the calm and the not so calm parts. School was a safe place for me. When I returned home after school, I learned to read the air as I walked into our house. If mother had a deep, crisp voice, I knew I better brace myself. The rest of the day was not going to be good. I knew there would be a lot of uncontrollable yelling. Once she started yelling, I tried to tune her out. I learned early on not to verbally respond to her questions while she was yelling. I would just stand before her with a blank, emotionless expression. I also knew when mother was having a good day, by the lilt in her voice. If her voice had a higher lilt, I knew I could finish my homework and go out and play.

Every day after school, my first question entering the front door was, "Is dad going to be home for dinner tonight?"

My dad worked late many nights and most of the day on Saturdays. There seemed to be more yelling and raging on the nights when dad was working late. I dreaded the many nights he worked late. Her yelling and ranting required me to apologize for things I didn't even know what I was apologizing for.

One of my favorite parts of the day was when I would wake up at 6:00 in the morning just to have breakfast with my father, before he had to leave for work. It was quiet, just dad and I. My dad was a big man, kind and caring. He was very handsome. I missed seeing him in the evenings.

I worked very hard in school, but it was difficult for me to focus on my teachers. I tried to pay attention. I loved school, it was my safe place and my mind could rest, so I would daydream. This was the time of the day when my brain felt the calmest. I felt safe and my body would instinctually relax from the pent-up stress. I didn't need to be on guard all the time. But this had a downside. I couldn't bring myself to a relaxed place and still be focused on when my teachers would teach. Oftentimes, I only grasped every third word they said. I thought I was following directions on assignments, but oftentimes I didn't. In those moments, when I could be still, I dreamed of a calmer life. I dreamed of the day when I didn't need to listen to the incessant yelling or flipping of behaviors. I dreamed of the day when I wouldn't have to be on guard all the time. Little did I know that working with people just like myself would be my life's work.

By third grade, my challenges with disorganization, a common trait among children in trauma, became a more noticeable issue. My brain was so tired most days, I just didn't understand what it meant to be organized. The concept of organization was foreign to me. I had no idea what I should do to become organized. To this day, organization is still a work in progress for me and requires deep concentration and focus.

Third grade is one of those grades of much change and some maturation. Children are exposed and held accountable to letter grades for the first time. One afternoon, when I was in third grade, I couldn't find one of my homework papers. I did the assigned work, I just couldn't find it. My teacher walked over to my desk and toppled it over in front of the whole class. The other kids laughed. "Now, maybe you can find that paper," she said and walked away.

I didn't like her much. Unlike my kindergarten to second grade teachers, this third-grade teacher didn't provide the calm or stability my other grade school teachers did. It was hard to have stress at home and at school. There was no respite that year. But I learned an important lesson that year that would resurface later in my life and provide me with decades of survival techniques. I learned the concept of balance that year. I learned that if one setting in your life is over the top stressful, then the other part of your life must be calm. I unconsciously learned and vowed that never again my life inside and outside my home would both have high degrees of ongoing stress at the same time. I was starting to understand the concept of balance.

Identifying children with trauma was not in the foreground like it is now. I was a high-energy child; therefore, the characteristics of trauma either weren't noticed or acknowledged by those around me. I worked hard to appear happy never showing my true feelings within. In time, I learned to regulate myself using a technique referred to as numbing. I became masterful, turning it off when I was around my dad and extended family and turning inward around my mother. I was never a behavior problem like many children with chronic, complex trauma. I loved the people around me and didn't want to be a problem to those that embraced me. While I was frequently confused, I didn't disassociate in a clinical way. I did often daydream about the field of criminology, but I was discouraged from believing that would ever be available to a woman. Little did I knew that selective numbing would become more challenging in time or that this skill set would prove instrumental in my career choice working with violence.

The ongoing lifelong challenge for me surfaced in the area of attachments. If someone doesn't feel safe to me, I run. The people I feel safe with are the lifelong loves in my life. It is hard to get close to me, but if someone is permitted into my tight circle, it is heartfelt and forever. For me, feeling a slight or a wrong is doubly wrong in my mind and that is always something I have to modulate. Sometimes a slight is just that and nothing more. It takes a little more self-talk for me to get through that. It is something I pray for on an ongoing basis; the ability to show grace and forgiveness. Yet, ironically and without my understanding, I don't intrinsically hold a grudge. If a relationship needs to be over, I just move on. I still have a small piece of my heart that still has pangs but overall, I am proud of how I have learned to dance through this complex issue in my life but if I am being honest, there are still moments of sadness in my heart. I have a wonderful family that I continue to be close with, and lifelong friends that I treasure. I actually feel grateful for the relationships in my life and move forward embracing those memories of them.

As I got into fourth and fifth grade mother hoped my tomboy ways would recede. They did not. My poor mother was so excited to have a daughter who would be beautiful like her and love dress up and enjoy experimenting with different types of makeup. She had a dream, an expectation and she did not get that in me. I often wished she would have had another baby girl so then maybe she would be happier. Once I even made up a story telling many neighbors my mother was pregnant. It wasn't so even though I wished it.

My dad would smile with a gleam in his eye and tell me I was the son he wanted. I played baseball, football, jumped off the roof playing superwoman, rode dirt bikes, and embraced my energetic side. My dad was a boxer in his early adult years. I think he'd laugh at how much his daughter, granddaughter, and great-granddaughters like wrestling and kick boxing!

Throughout my childhood, I loved playing pickup games of kickball or baseball, and sometimes-even football. When I was eleven years old, mother tried to forbid me to play sports any more. She said it was inappropriate for me to be playing those games with the boys. She used to tell me that when a girl plays sports with the boys, she's asking for sex. I just wanted to play ball. I have never understood her connections with sports being somehow related to sex. I just wanted to win.

"If you are going to act like a boy, you are going to look like a boy," mother said in disgust. She took a medium sized, plastic gold bowl and put it on my head. Then she took out the scissors and cut my hair short, like a boy. She kept my hair like that until I was in sixth grade. It was a good thing the Buster Brown haircuts were trendy. Unfortunately, this short haircut did not hide my large ears. The kids in my neighborhood didn't say much, but my classmates made mean comments. I was humiliated by this haircut. When I looked at the other girls with long hair and I would promise myself that one day I will have hair like them. And to this day, my hair has always remained long.

As I entered the adolescent stage, mother would tell me what a mess I looked like all the time. Frequently, she would shake her head and go tell me to do something with myself.

When I made the cheerleading squad in middle school and the freshman year of high school, I realized she was wrong. I believed cheerleaders had to be pretty and they selected me. That was the first memory I had of feeling empowered.

Turning twelve was memorable. Besides getting my period, there were two other initiations into adulthood. The first was mother dressing me up like a Playboy Bunny on dad's birthday. She said it would give him a big surprise when he walked in the door.

Mother was excited. We'd never played dress up before. She put makeup on me and took great pains to make sure I looked perfect. When dad walked through the door, we yelled, "Happy Birthday!"

Mother gave me a gentle push forward and exclaimed, "See, we dressed her up like a bunny for your birthday." Dad was furious. He never got angry. I had only seen him this angry once before, when we returned home early from a family vacation at a dude ranch.

Mother sat in the back seat, which wasn't typical, and I sat upfront with dad. Mother was yelling, "You have made a fool of me. You will never do that again!" I had no idea what was going on but he raised his voice and told her, "Enough!" Dad wouldn't talk to her again for the remainder of the four-hour ride home. I later learned that my dad had casually spoken to a woman near the horse barn.

While I thought, my family looked totally normal to others, I often felt confused. I was dressed up for dad's birthday celebration. Mother said dad would be happy. He clearly wasn't happy. He took me to the bathroom, told me to wipe off all of the makeup and change my clothes immediately.

We didn't celebrate dad's birthday that night. We never spoke of that incident again. I didn't understand the significance of this, until I was older. I thought I had ruined his birthday celebration and felt badly about that.

One night, that same year, mother asked me to stay in the kitchen to talk to her while she was clearing the dinner dishes. Sometimes we had talks after dinner. Dad was always working late when she brought these inappropriate topics up.

She told me that sometimes she finds dad too heavy to be on top, so there are other creative ways to "perform," as she called it. Now she was on top, but she didn't like it as much. I had no idea how to respond to her. "Ok" was always a safe response with mother. I'm not sure if I understood what she was talking about at that time.

I'm also not sure if I thought we were like all the other families on the street or I had to convince myself of that for survival. I was truly happy playing baseball, reading, and being outside with my friends. Years later, I was told that my mother saw my playing sports as a sort of sexual stimulation. She claims this gave her an indication I was ready for such a conversation that I definitely was not ready for. She felt I was ready to talk about playing spin the bottle and seven minutes of heaven. To me, heaven was playing sports. I was not interested, but she planned a sixth-grade party for my classmates. After about two hours, after our BBQ was devoured, she invited everyone to the basement where she invited everyone to play spin the bottle. She reviewed the instructions then went upstairs. If you were at my sixth-grade party, I apologize and I am mortified.

Throughout my adolescence, I tried to be a non-entity in my house, especially when dad was gone. Invisible would describe it accurately. School was a place I could step out and find myself a bit.

Towards the end of ninth grade, my parents announced we would be moving at the beginning of the summer. They were excited about driving west for a new adventure. They gleefully celebrated the abstract notion that we would drive until we found a place we liked somewhere in the western part of the United States. They had no idea where that would be. I hid my panic about leaving the safety of my neighborhood, my grandmothers, aunts, uncles, and cousins. I loved them. This is my first memory of my life being totally turned upside down and I felt very insecure and unsafe leaving everyone who I felt safe with. Now all I had was my dad and my dog, Fawn.

I frequently asked my parents if they had any idea where we would be going so I could quell some of my fears. Mother told me our new home would be somewhere in California, Arizona, or New Mexico. This panic set off a mild rebellious phase inside of me.

A few months before our scheduled move, mother accused me of stealing liquor from the family's small liquor cabinet. Allegedly, I was drinking the vodka. Mother continued to rant that she could see there was less and less vodka every time she went to the cabinet. I didn't drink. I tried to make her believe me, but she didn't.

Her relentless accusations of me stealing and drinking continued to go on for years, even after we moved. Ironically, I never liked liquor, not as a teenager, nor as an adult. I just tried to ignore the allegations so as to not give her more need to provoke her to rage. Over time, it wore me down. Dad heard the accusations that I was stealing vodka a few times. He'd just shake his head and smile. I never knew what that meant.

I actually became rebellious a few months before we moved somewhere out west. I was scared to death to leave my family and close-knit neighborhood. I couldn't understand why we were uncertain about where we would be moving. I did not share my parent's enthusiasm about this exciting adventure. I believe this started a new path in my life's journey. I was going to feel even more unsafe than I had been feeling previously. I was fourteen years old and made a promise to myself, I was going to become independent and learn to support myself. And I did just that, emancipating just three years later, during my seventeenth year.

We were going to drive out west, look for a house, and my parents would look for work. Not excited, I started hanging around with a different crowd of friends in my hometown. My grades were still strong, I was still a cheerleader, but I started hanging around a broader group, one that I never would have associated with if we stayed in our home town. We experimented with several of the thrills introduced to adolescents in the 1970's. Mother didn't have to worry about drinking. It was definitely not an interest of mine. My rebellion was satisfied with a new behavior, getting high on weed and hash. It was an escape I craved and it brought me peace.

One Saturday, I told mother I was going to the mall with friends, a new independent behavior for me at fourteen years old. She reminded me to be back by 5pm. She and dad were meeting relatives in the city for dinner. I didn't respond, I just walked out the door. That afternoon, I did go to the mall, but not with the friends I told her I was with. I went with my other group of friends. We hitchhiked to the mall and planned to hitchhike back. I thought hitchhiking was exciting. I got a rush at the danger I placed myself in during this phase. "Rush" another concept I was able to later relate to in my work with high risk youth violence. 'Feeding the rush in a positive way' was a technique I revisited later, personally and as well as with clients.

Getting someone to pick us up late on a Saturday afternoon was harder than we thought. I didn't get home until after six o'clock. I was very late.

Mother greeted me at the door. "Where were you?" she asked.

"At the mall," I responded, walking toward the stairs that led to my room. "We missed the bus," I flippantly added. This was the first time I had tried to dismiss her comments. She grabbed me and pulled me into the living room, a few steps away.

"You are lying to me. You weren't with your friend, Andrea. She called to see where you were, so obviously, you weren't with her. Do a better job getting your story straight."

She lifted her hand to get ready to slap me in the face. I grabbed it just before it landed. "Don't you ever touch me," I said looking her straight in the eye, then dropping her hand like I was letting go of a glass about to break all over the floor. I climbed the stairs to my room. This was the first time I had ever challenged her.

"You are grounded for a month," she yelled after me.

I ignored her. "Well, if that isn't enough, I'm grounding you from cheerleading as well."

That made me turn around. I was so proud of being a cheerleader. I had practiced my splits, cartwheels, and herkies for hours trying to perfect them so they looked more natural. In reality, they did not come natural or easy to me. They actually took a great deal of effort.

Practicing for cheerleading was another saving grace for me. It gave me time with a nice group of girls. I liked my new friends and loved my new outlet. Mother knew that cheerleading was the one thing that meant a lot to me at that time in my life. So that was what she was going to take away. Little did I realize at that time, she was on the lookout for my vulnerabilities. This was the first memory I have of her holding something that was special to me as a manipulative hostage.

She smiled with her eyes looking like a shark, "So that's what will get you, the cheerleading." That is the first memory I have of her shark eyes. I studied them well.

"If I miss a month, I'm off the team," I said with less confidence than I'd had a moment before.

"Cheerleading and school, that's it, otherwise you are in the house for a month." She backed down. That was not something I'd ever seen before nor would I see again.

It was a month of hell. I read a lot of books and got lost in them oftentimes wishing I could be one of the characters in a book with a happy ending.

I resumed school, cheerleading, and stopped associating with my other group of friends. I settled in for my last remaining months at home, without any more rebellion, just a continual panic about what would lie ahead.

Chapter Four:

Sweet Sixteen, Not So Sweet

Mother always dreamed of my Sweet Sixteen birthday party. She planned for it, much like a parent plans for a wedding. Sadly, for mother, she didn't have a daughter who shared her same excitement.

I'd always dreaded my birthday. The only thing I looked forward to was spending time with my dad on my birthday each year.

He would make it a special day, taking me out to lunch, just dad and I Every year, we would go to our favorite restaurant, The Steakhouse in Huntington.

We'd order the wedge salad even before it became popular. The waiter always brought a carousel of dressings to put on the table and we could pick whichever one we wanted. I always considered all of the choices, yet always selected my childhood favorite, French dressing.

Our lunch included dessert at the end of this enormous meal. We made our own sundaes. Dad and I would laugh as we talked about what toppings we wanted for our scoop of ice cream. Sometimes, we'd pick all of them.

Every year, after lunch, dad would take me to the mall and every year, I would pick out a little trinket or memento for mother. I would give it to her after returning home from my birthday lunch.

It was my way of saying, "Thank you for having me." I was trying to make her see, it was her special day too, not just mine. But she was never very happy on those days.

By the time my sixteenth birthday was approaching, I had only lived in our new Scottsdale home for less than a year. I was just starting my fourth high school in two years. We moved around a lot as my parents decided where to ultimately buy a house. Getting settled out west over the summer turned into an ordeal that lasted well over a year.

I couldn't try out for cheerleading at any of the three high schools I attended since I continually missed tryouts each time we'd move. My parent's priority was enrolling me before the first day of school. My tryouts for sports or participation in clubs, was not a priority for them. They were in their own world, enthusiastic about their ongoing new adventure.

I started at so many different high schools within such a short time that it was difficult to make close friends. Those were the years I was more introspective and spent a lot of time alone, reading, writing, and taking walks. I never felt happy during that period of my life. I missed my friends from back home, the place I had lived for the first fourteen years of my life.

Arizona just never felt like home to me. During those two years, I felt like I was flying on the peripheral, trying to make a landing, but not quite able to execute it.

A few weeks before my birthday, Mother came to me breathless and enthusiastic about my party. Apparently, 'we' were changing the theme of my Sweet Sixteen Birthday from a formal event to a hayride and BBQ. Once again, I looked at her with a totally blank expression.

"Well, I thought you'd be happier. Show a little appreciation and excitement for crying out loud." Poor mother. She was frustrated. Not only did she have a tomboy for a daughter, I did not have friends, or any desire to get excited about parties or fashion. I was comfortable wearing a pair of jeans, a tank top, and my hair in braids. I definitely did not fit her vision of a daughter who was also her best friend and confidant, as she had shared with relatives right after my birth.

If she and I were classmates or neighbors living on the same street, I don't think we would have been friends. Our interests and perspectives were just too divergent.

Looking down, I told her I didn't have enough friends to invite to a big birthday party like that.

"Of course, you do!" she insisted. "Sit right down here and come up with thirty-five names. You must know thirty-five people!"

"How about a quiet family celebration at a nice restaurant?" I suggested praying she would allow me this. She did not.

"We are having a hayride for thirty-five people. There will be a bonfire followed by everyone coming back here. Your father will have a lovely BBQ and your friends can swim in the pool."

"Mother, please," I begged, "I do not have thirty-five people to invite." "Well then you will have to sit here until you do."

I wrote names of people I hardly knew just to get away from the table.

"See, was that so hard?" she smiled with delight.

Mother carried on with her party planning, indifferent to my frequent requests preferring a small family dinner at a restaurant rather than this big extravaganza.

"I will get the invitations later today and you can hand them out at school tomorrow. Remember to emphasize to each person that an RSVP is very important. We need to know how much food to buy."

I'd thought we were done, but then mother added, "Be sure to get each person's phone numbers. That is a must when you are giving out birthday invitations for a celebration like this."

Throughout the next few days, I dutifully handed out the invitations as mother demanded. I asked each of those invited for their phone number. I tried not to notice the constant confusion on the faces of these people I hardly knew. It was embarrassing.

The day of the party arrived and only five people had responded that they were coming to the birthday celebration.

Mother was furious. "How come the other thirty people have not called? Don't they realize I have food ordered?"

I prayed six o'clock would not come that day. I was somehow hoping the entire evening could be skipped in its entirety. I wished there was a fast forward button.

The five people who had RSVP'd actually attended the party. They seemed excited about the night ahead. I was desperately trying to do the same.

We were supposed to arrive at the ranch by 6:30 for the hayride. We waited for the other guests to arrive, but by 6:30, no one else came.

"Give me that list of the people you invited. They are so rude. Who do they think they are not showing up? I want you call every single one of them and ask them why they are late. Tell them to hurry up and get here, we can't wait much longer."

"Let's just go have fun with the five people who are here," I pleaded.

"Absolutely not, get on that phone and start calling," mother demanded. She stood over me as I called each person.

Many didn't answer, thank goodness. A few parents answered and said their children weren't home. Fortunately, I was only able to reach a few people from the invitation list.

Mother could be heard yelling in the background, "How could they do this to me? Don't they understand what they have put me through?"

About half an hour later, Dad finally stepped in and re-directed me. "Come outside," he said softly.

I went with him and the others waiting in the car. He drove us to the ranch. It took everything in me not to burst into tears at the embarrassment, humiliation, and degradation I felt that night.

Two days later, it was all I could do to return to school. The week after the party disaster, I made myself a Sweet Sixteen birthday promise of my own. I would do everything I could to get out of that house as fast as I could.

The very next month, I enrolled at a community college near our house. I signed up for two classes. One was a 100 level English Class and the other was a Philosophy Class. I had a lot of trouble with the Philosophy Class. As hard as I tried, I just wasn't a deep thinker. I tried, but my mind was like a blank slate.

Every day, I would go to high school until 2pm then I would drive over to the community college for the remainder of the afternoon. I worked most evenings and weekends. Between all those commitments, I was not home much. I believed that advancing my education, being involved in clubs and student council, and volunteering at a children's hospital were going to be part of the ticket to get myself out of this hell at home.

My last high school was part of the new open school concept. It was considered a progressive school. I liked this school and I made friends.

Sometime after my birthday fiasco, I became involved with student council and held various positions on the school newspaper. Sometimes, when we were struggling with tight layout deadlines, we would all get together on a Saturday afternoon and finish the layouts. Many perceived this as a stressful task; for me, I thought it was fun. That was the first time in the two years since we'd moved that I felt a part of something. It felt natural and provided some of the calm I'd experienced with those I missed from back home.

I became very structured, making sure my grades were strong in both high school and community college. I found pockets of my day to be involved with extra-curricular activities and I saved almost all my money. I received several academic scholarships and for the first time, I became excited about my future.

I knew once I left, I never would go back and I never did.

Chapter Five:

Virginity Confirmed

As I walked in the door from school one afternoon, several months after my birthday party, mother announced, "Don't get too comfortable. We are turning right around and leaving. You have an appointment."

"I do?" I struggled to remember.

I was a mature sixteen-year-old and meticulous about scheduling my appointments since my days were so tightly orchestrated. I was juggling high school, student council, high school newspaper as the assistant editor, taking college classes, and working two jobs, along with volunteer work. For part of that time, I was also the teen correspondent for the Arizona Republic Newspaper trying to meet strict deadlines.

"Yes, you do," She curtly responded. "And you will drive." Mother hated to drive.

I started my red push-button Dodge Dart and asked "Where are we going?"

"I made you an appointment with my gynecologist. You've been having cramps right before your period and I want to make sure everything is okay down there."

Before I could even respond, she added, "You can tell me the truth, if you are having sex with that young man you have been dating, tell me now," she demanded. "Sex could be the reason for your cramps."

"I'm not, I'm really not! I swear!" I repeated that several times hoping she would cancel the appointment, but she did not.

What was she even talking about, having sex? I was one of the last girls to think about that. I didn't have many friends, let alone boyfriends. I was casually dating a guy my parents approved of. Our big night out was a movie and a hamburger.

I dutifully did what I was told and drove to the doctor's office. Once inside I was frenetic and felt like I was ready to explode. What was happening here? When we got to the doctor's office, mother filled out the paperwork. I have no idea what she wrote.

When they called my name, mother escorted me into the examining room. My trepidation increased with each step I took towards that room.

"Oh darn," she said once we were alone in the room. "I should have told you to change your clothes. Too bad you wore a dress today; pants and a shirt would have made this procedure so much easier. Now you will have to take everything off."

"Everything?" I asked, my eyes wide open with terror.

"Absolutely everything," she said with a half-smile.

The nurse had left without giving me a gown or a paper sheet to drape over myself. I slipped out of my clothes slowly.

"Hurry up!" she barked, "We don't want to keep the doctor waiting."

She sat in the seat to the side of the examination table as I took off the last of my clothes. After I had completed the task of total nakedness, I sat on the table. I felt cold even though it was over 90 degrees outside.

She started examining my naked body with her eyes, commenting about the changes she was noticing since she had last seen me naked, many years before. I felt dirty. The doctor came in quickly and pulled two metal handles out from the bottom of the table. I'd never seen anything like those. I was frozen.

"Come on now, feet in those stirrups and scoot your bottom to the edge of this table." Before I could even follow his instructions, he took both of his hands on the inside of my knees and shoved my legs apart. The door to the examining room opened at that same time, and two nurses walked into the room to observe.

He inserted something cold and hard inside me. I later learned it was called a speculum. I was so mortified that I tried to get outside of my body. I could hear mother in the background directing me to take big deep breaths. I was absolutely traumatized at the things he continued to do to my body and felt violated.

After he finished groping everywhere and removed his hand from 'down there', mother ordered me to put my clothes on and go wait for her in the car. "I am going to speak to the doctor and nurses in private now," she informed me. They all waited as I haphazardly put on my clothes, buttoning as I was walking out the door.

I did as I was told. I was furious. Once again, I felt humiliated. That was the first time I felt raw hatred towards my mother. I knew I had to squash my emotions when she came into the car or it would be worse. I don't know how long I remained in the car. I lost all sense of time.

When mother returned to the car, she took a few moments to get herself settled in. I turned on the ignition. She turned to stare at me. "Please put on your seatbelt," was all I could think of to say.

She directed me to drive to the drug store. As we were driving, she announced, "You should be glad the doctor was able to tell me that you are still a virgin."

I had absolutely no response for her. I no longer felt dirty, I felt filthy. I felt like an object, not a person. Mother had no compunction about how I felt. It was as simple as that.

That day, like many, I learned to control the boiling that was going on inside of me. I'd become a master at controlling my emotions. It was like a mantra going on inside my head, "Do not let your emotions show. Do not feel. Do not even flinch or she will come in for the kill."

What did I feel at that time? Absolutely nothing and everything. I know that was one of the moments I hated my mother the most in my life. Survival amplified my feeling of numbness. I felt sexually violated, having absolutely no idea why that had just happened. I remember I did not feel like a person. There was no conversation about sexuality, about love making with another person, just the verbal reminder that if I really want a man to have fantastic sex with me, I should fight hard to keep my legs closed and make him work for it. I will always remember her telling me it will make him like it more.

I don't believe I had any understanding of how a mother should protect their child, at that time. I'm not sure I was capable of processing that much. I was on survival mode, counting the days. I didn't know my mother had a personality disorder. I just knew she was the enemy and I had to get away. This incident, like many was filed in the black box inside my mind. Later as a criminologist, I would learn that what I was doing was compartmentalizing. It was only later, after I had children that I thought about this day. A parent instinctually protects their child, don't they? That was a natural feeling I carry with me to this day, protecting my family. I did not feel that as a child, not with my mother. Later in life, difficult as it was, I could not escape admitting to myself, that for whatever reasons, my father did not protect me against my mother. I am not sure if he didn't know because he was seldom home. I do not recall a time when he directly witnessed her raging at me or disconcerting behavior except during the bunny incident. My mother told me right before she passed away, that one of the last things my father said to her before he went mute was he was furious that the reason their daughter didn't visit much was because mother drove me away. I did not respond to that comment when she said it. Silence was often my response with her, but her comment was correct. In my heart, I always wished I could talk to my mother like other daughters did with their mothers. I never did achieve this.

Mother's voice brought me out of my introspection. I forced myself to breathe, reassuring myself I only had a few more months of living at home and concentrated on visualizing my future. "You are almost there I would tell myself." Until then, I was at her mercy.

I drove us to the pharmacy and waited in the car. She returned with a pack of little yellow pills that came in a dial instead of a bottle like other prescriptions.

"These will help you with your cramps. Take one every morning before you go to school. I will be checking to make sure you take them."

I did not question mother. I just wanted to get home, go in my room, listen to Simon and Garfunkel, and shrivel up. I told mother I was too sick to eat dinner that night.

Two years later, when I was in college and decided to have sex with my boyfriend, I decided to make an appointment at Planned Parenthood. I was proud of myself for being responsible, making sure I had birth control before we had sex.

This time, I was ready for the exam. Inside the examining room, the metal stirrups were covered with cooking mitts. The room was decorated with affirmations and informative posters. The room was painted a soft pastel and I felt relaxed. Before the nurse practitioner came into the office, the medical assistant asked me a series of questions.

The first series of questions were about medications I was presently taking. I handed the dial of the pills I had been taking for the past two years to the assistant. She looked at me perplexed.

"Do you want a refill on your prescription?" I told her that was not the reason for my appointment. I explained, I wanted to start having sex and needed to get on birth control. She finished the interview and left to tell the nurse practitioner that I was ready. My dial of pills was still on the counter.

The nurse practitioner came in. She was a patient, middle-aged woman, and an advocate for women's health. I knew I was in good hands and loved the atmosphere and services Planned Parenthood offered.

After the exam, she calmly asked me, "Do you know what these pills are that you have been taking?"

"My mother put me on them two years ago to help my cramps." I responded earnestly. Even though this lovely practitioner didn't know my background, she gathered something was definitely amiss here.

She gently touched my hand, "Sue, you have been taking birth control pills for two years. That's what these are."

I explained to her that about a year before I had asked my mother whether these were birth control pills. Mother told me they weren't real birth control pills, they just looked like them. They prevented cramps but would not prevent pregnancy.

"This prescription is real and these are full strength birth control pills," she explained to me. I was mortified. She refilled my prescription with a repeat of the instructions I had already been following.

As I walked away from that appointment, I was confused. There was a sadness that permeated deep inside me. I remembered vividly the day mother took me to her gynecologist. She lied to me. She had me examined to see if I was a virgin.

Once again, I felt violated by my mother. This was the second time I felt such deep hatred toward her. To this day, I cannot comprehend how a mother can do this to her daughter.

I never spoke of this to anyone, not to my father, not to a friend, and surely not to my mother. Instead, the next day, I signed up to be a volunteer at Planned Parenthood.

Chapter Six:

Validation of A Rape

"Of course, you were raped. When you walk around like a slut and dress like a slut, you ask for it, and you deserve it."

My brain was trying to comprehend my mother's response when I shared with her that I had been sexually assaulted with a gun to my head. I knew better than to share this but I honestly needed my mother at that moment.

Bringing myself back to reality, "What did you just say?" I asked with a disgusted tone she wasn't used to.

I had emancipated several months before, shortly after my early graduation from high school, at the age of seventeen. I was starting school at Arizona State University and came home for three days in between my trip abroad and starting college.

For the past several months, I had been living in the Middle East working on an agricultural commune near Haifa in Israel. I didn't know any one there. I had read about an opportunity to work and travel with minimal expenses in Israel. The brochure just called out to me and within forty-eight hours of receiving it, I submitted my application.

Selling my Dodge Dart for the airfare, most of my other expenses were minimal. Since we were working for room and board, I had a little extra money for incidentals. Dad slipped me a hundred dollars as he was hugging me goodbye at the airport. I look back at that scene of two parents seeing off their newly emancipated seventeen- year old and supporting a trip to the war torn Middle East. I can't imagine my children following in those footsteps at seventeen. I'm glad they didn't have to.

The experience was amazing, getting up every day at 4am, grabbing a quick cup of coffee, and jumping into pickups that drove us out to the orchards to pick grapes, oranges, and other fruits and vegetables.

Since it was so hot, generally 118 degrees, we started early each day and ended by 2 in the afternoon. The remainder of the afternoons and evenings were ours to spend however we wanted to. Sometimes, we went to different beaches. Once we climbed Mt. Masada. One of my favorites was shopping at the art galleries in Safad.

I was fascinated by the culture in the Middle East, the dress, the way the women carried themselves, and the military obligations. I loved to sit in the parks in the cities and just watch the people. I was impressed with their ability to balance between strength and humility and amazed by the commitments of both the men and women to serve in the military after high school. The respect and honor those in the military displayed, moved me in a way I had never been touched before.

I found the camaraderie between those in the military and on the compounds so intrinsically rich. It had been a long time since I had felt like that. I believe I would not have returned home if I did not have a four- year academic scholarship waiting for me. My practical self, continued to tell me I was foolish to throw away such an amazing academic opportunity. My emotional self, did not want to leave.

We were a group of new found friends, young women coming together from all over the world; working and traveling. We got to know each other well as we shared months of living together, working together, and traveling together.

There were eleven other single women, like me. We came from many different cultures, yet we blended into our group. More than just sharing one big dorm room, we shared life changing experiences. Living in a country in war was never something I got used to, but the connectedness was.

We filled six bunk beds and six miniature armoires. In total, we were several hundred -people living all together in our communal compound setting. Each family was given a small house, with one bedroom, a sitting area, and a very small kitchen. It was barely big enough to cook a meal. That wasn't a problem since everyone ate in the communal dining halls. All the children slept in the children's house which provided great protection by the adults. They felt it easier to keep their children safe by housing them all together than having them spread out.

They assured me that the parents and children spent more time together than their counterparts in the United States. When parents were done with work and children were done with school, all inside the compound walls, the families spent quality time together for the remainder of the afternoon, through the dinner hour and evening. While fascinating and definitely practical and safe, I still had trouble wrapping my head around that.

I was fascinated with the Israeli culture. I took too many chances while I was there, allowing my curiosity to overrule my good judgment sometimes.

As I was approaching the Dome of the Rock located in Old Jerusalem, I saw a funeral procession. Six men were carrying a simple coffin. I noticed there were only men in the funeral procession.

"Where were the women?" I asked myself.

Impulsive and curious, I went closer. Two men came running at me holding light blue sheet like material. I was not sure where they came from. They were yelling. I did not understand them.

One man wrapped the sheet around my shoulders and another around my head. I naively had no idea that the long shorts and tee shirt I was wearing revealed too much skin. I learned a lot about respecting other cultures that day.

Later, after an afternoon of shopping, I grabbed a falafel, a new favorite of mine. As always, I boarded the crowded bus, I thought, "Lucky for me, I made it on the bus." Many people had to wait for the next bus.

There were two soldiers sitting at the front of each side of the bus holding guns. That was a common sight on the buses in Israel. Even though it was part of everyday life there, I never got used to that either.

Since the bus was so crowded, there was only room for me to stand in the aisle and grab the ceiling rail as the bus moved.

Once the bus lurched forward, I tightened my grip. As I looked down, I noticed there was a soldier sitting next to me. He had a cast from just below his knee to his toes.

He looked up as I almost lost my balance. I was a little embarrassed and smiled at him. He offered me his seat. I told him I thought he needed the seat more than I did. We both laughed.

As we headed north, the bus started clearing out little by little. A seat became available across from this handsome soldier. I took it. He told me he was in the Israeli Military stationed fifteen minutes north of where

I was working. He had gone to Haifa for supplies and meetings, and was now returning to his base.

"I'd like to invite you to take a dinner with me." He said. "Are you free tomorrow night?" I was quiet as I considered this invitation.

"The bus returns in the opposite direction at 6:15 tomorrow night. If you say yes, I will be on the bus waiting for you as you get on."

He seemed like a gentleman, respectful, and interesting. I knew I wanted to continue talking with him. He interrupted my thoughts; "I will take you to my favorite restaurant in Haifa."

I thought about safety. I really did. I thought he was injured and I could outrun him. My gut told me to be cautious but I did not listen. Besides, we were taking a bus. I laughed, chastising myself for being paranoid, all the while forgetting to appreciate the gift of fear or trusting the voice in my gut.

I was a world traveler. That meant not being afraid to meet new people, right? I dismissed the voice inside. After a brief pause, I accepted his invitation.

As promised, he was waiting for me the next evening when I boarded the bus. He was wearing his military uniform and even though he was off duty he still carried his gun. We went to a simple restaurant. He told me their specialty was lamb. After dinner, we walked around Haifa for a little while. What a magnificent city at night, full of lights and people laughing in the park. I loved it.

After a short while, he asked me if I'd be willing to go with him to his office headquarters. He needed to get more ammo for his gun. He explained, in earnest, that he'd forgotten to get enough ammo when he came to Haifa the day before. He added he wouldn't be returning to Haifa again for at least another week. I agreed to this seemingly harmless request. It made sense to me at the time, but I was also only seventeen without much experience.

We approached several rows of buildings. I could see the windows did not have glass. Instead they had blinds or a shutter like covering. Almost all of them were tightly sealed. I knew this had something to do with one of the precautionary measures associated with war and bombs.

We went into what he referred to as the first- floor office. It looked more like an apartment to me. The living room had a large desk in it, so

I rationalized that the apartment had been made into an office of sorts. There was a couch, a few small chairs, and a television.

He excused himself into what I ignorantly thought was the other office. He asked me to wait in the living room. I did. As I looked around this main room, I noticed it was sparsely decorated so there wasn't much to look at.

Moments later he reappeared. His pants were completely off of his good leg and bunched around his leg with the cast. He had wrapped his pants around the thigh of his casted leg. I saw a gun pointed at my face as he approached me. I backed up towards the door.

"That won't work," he chuckled, holding up a large key. "Our doors lock from the inside and you need the key to get out." I'd never heard of such a thing. But again, I was only seventeen and thought I was worldlier than I was.

He grabbed my long hair, pulling me towards that other room.

"Please," I told him, "I have never done this before. I don't want my first time to be this way. I don't want this to be the memory of my first time." I thought he'd take pity on me and let me go.

"Then we will do this a different way," he commanded, his demeanor nothing like the friendly soldier I had enjoyed on the bus.

He pulled me towards the bed in the other room, and pushed me to my knees. He sat on the bed pointing the gun at my temple. He pushed my head down and said, "Open your mouth and make me think you love doing this or you will get a bullet through your head."

He pushed my head further down to fill my mouth with all of him. I had never done anything like this before. It was very difficult not to gag.

I wondered if he would really shoot me. I decided not to find out the answer to that question. I was in survival mode, once again. I'd never seen a blow job before and had no idea how to make him "think I like it".

Movies and television shows in the 1970's never showed such things. I tried not to think about what I was doing and let my mind drift away from the experience my body was having. When he was done, he demanded I swallow. I thought about it, I just could not and spit his secretions all over the floor.

I got up quickly. I saw through the corner of my eye he had placed the key on the nightstand. It was within my reach. I am not sure when he put it there. I grabbed it and ran to the apartment door. My hands were shaking as I tried to fit the key in the lock. I could hear him shuffling up behind me. I truly believed he might kill me.

I wasn't sure if the gun was still in his hand since my back was to him. My heart was beating so fast that I felt like I couldn't breathe. He walked up behind me, turned me around, and did the most unexpected thing. He hugged me.

There were tears in his eyes as he apologized over and over. "I was told girls from the United States are easy and like to have lots of sex."

"Well not this one. I'm not easy and I've never had sex," I responded with more confidence than I actually felt.

I was not going to let him see me cry. "You need to let me leave now," I demanded and shockingly, he did.

Once I made my way out, I just ran toward the lights in the center of town. It felt like I ran for miles. I have no idea how long I ran. I saw a cab, got in, and asked the driver to take me back to my residence.

When I returned to the dorm, I grabbed my towel, and headed to the bathroom where I repeatedly threw up.

One of the single male workers, who lived in the men's dorm nearby, heard me crying. When he approached the bathroom door, I was throwing up.

He came into the bathroom, slowly walked towards me, grabbed the towel from my hands and gently washed my face and my hands.

He went to the communal kitchen and brought me back a hot cup of tea. Then he led me to a place under a tree near the dorms and held me as I cried. He never asked what happened.

"It's ok," he kept stroking my hair. "You are safe."

Eventually, I told him what happened and how dirty I felt. I continued to ask myself how I could have been so gullible and foolish. My friend just held me. Sometime that night, he walked me to the dorm door, hugged me good night, and I went to sleep.

The next morning and every morning after, I made believe this assault never happened.

I thought to myself. "I am strong. I can get past this. He may have invaded my body, but I wasn't going to allow him to touch my soul."

I hid this event in the black box of my memory, like so many other incidents both before and after. That was not hard for me to do.

Several months later, when I returned to my parent's home in the United States, I told my mother what had happened. I did not tell my father. Maybe she did.

I'm not sure what I expected from my mother after I told her about my sexual assault. Yet again, her response was not one I wouldn't have expected even with her history, "Of course you were raped. When you walk around like a slut and dress like a slut, you ask for it, and you deserve it." I was hoping this would be the moment when she would step into the role of the mother. She did not. Instead I chastised myself that I was so vulnerable and ruminated over why I let my wall down.

I looked right at her, turned around, and left. Maybe, all I really needed from my mother was just a hug.

As I have reflected on this event from my youth, I don't know what was worse, the sexual assault or my mother's reaction. I never went for counseling after this incident. The only other person I ever told about this was my mother. I was numb after her response.

When I registered for my undergraduate classes, I was required to select a physical education class. I chose judo and remained with the practice for several years. I only stopped practicing judo on a steady basis once I earned my brown belt. Little did I know that judo would provide me with yet another skillset. Judo provided me yet another prong of empowerment and offered me a sense of confidence even with the most challenging intense confrontations.

Sometime during my freshman year at the university, and a few months after the assault, I trained as a victim advocate with the Center Against Sexual Assault in Phoenix. I also became a college campus presenter at seminars, teaching coeds how to stay safe from assault. I continued to try to make something positive out of something negative.

The irony is that I still remember what I was wearing on the day of my assault, a long blue and green halter dress. It came down to my ankles. I also wore a sweater over my halter dress. Contrary to my mother's 'spewing' that I dressed like a slut, I always kept it buttoned up.

Chapter Seven:

To Escort or Not to Escort

"Remember, you need to be on time, 3:15 sharp! They are expecting you." Mother reminded me for the second time.

I wrote the address down on a slip of paper and promised I would wear the short white skirt, the black, low cut scoop neck shirt, and high-heels. Mother insisted this would land me the job.

"And wear your hair down," she added before hanging up.

I found that a bit unusual. She always yelled at me to do something with the mop of hair on my head. She used to ridicule me that my hair was always a mess.

"You have to cover those ears of yours. They are way too big for your face," she added yet again, before hanging up. There was always a dig before she would hang-up. I never did get used to that. She called back a few moments later, for the third time.

"I forgot to tell you, it is similar to what you are doing now, but the pay is better. Remember what I told you. Be confident, let yourself shine at this interview and you will definitely get the job."

I drove to a small one- story tract home on the other side of town. There were tie-died blankets hanging over the windows and a few beat-up cars and one nice car in the driveway.

This time, my intuition told me to pay more attention to this situation. All of this was preparation for my life as a criminologist and situational awareness.

This didn't look like a place for a job interview, yet my own mother wouldn't send me to a place that was unsafe, I initially thought, but this time the instinct came blaring in and I was ready for whatever was on the other side of that door.

Mothers protect and nurture their children. At nineteen, I still could not accept that unlike other mothers, my mother was not nurturing or protective of her child. Yet, I always held out hope that for one day she would show me that warm side of her. I did not know she was incapable of fulfilling my one wish until I was in my forties.

I knocked on the front door and someone shouted, "Come in."

When I walked into the living room, no one was there. So, I just stood there looking at the bare walls and worn out couch.

A middle-aged man came out and asked me to sit down.

"I'll be right back," he said.

He returned a short time later with a middle-aged lady close to his same age. Neither of them were especially memorable looking.

I stood up to shake their hands, as I'd been taught to do when I met new people. Before I could sit back down on the couch, the woman asked me to turn around and bend over, as though I were picking something up from the floor.

I thought that was a weird request for a job interview. I did sense something was wrong, I just didn't know exactly what. I was no longer naive and trusting, regardless that my mother arranged for this interview.

"Ok, be seated," the man said. "You realize you must be discreet. Are you able to do that?"

"I believe so," I answered hesitantly, not sure at this point what he was talking about.

"You must also make yourself available any night of the week that we might need you." the woman added.

At the time of this interview, I was working as a cocktail waitress at a popular disco club in our college town. I never had to make myself available every night of the week. Sometimes, one of the managers would ask if I wanted to pick up another shift if someone called in sick, but I never had to be available seven nights a week.

Immediately, I had an uneasy feeling in the pit of my stomach. I decided to stop the misdirected self-talk going on inside my head. This was what it was, and it just felt odd and I was not going to get caught up again in 'more crazy'.

As the interview, continued, I was invited to ask them any questions I had. I asked if they could tell me more about the job.

They smiled at each other, amused by my question. Both seemed a bit unclear and looked at me confused. The woman snickered, "Why did you come in for this interview?"

"My mother told me about this job. She made the appointment for me. She told me this was a great paying job." I sounded like a child, a foolish, impish child. Thinking about this after the fact made me sick.

"You will be escorting businessmen," she answered after a long silence. She was staring straight at me trying to read my face. "Do you understand what this means?"

I put my head down and muttered quietly, "I have early morning classes and I cannot work late every night." I don't think she heard me. The room got quiet. I stood up.

"I'm sorry to have taken up your time, "I whispered. "I do not think I am right for this job," I said as I walked out.

I ran to my car, starting it with an urgency that wasn't really there, except for the anxiety inside of me. I pulled away quickly though I was not in a rush.

A few miles down the road, I pulled my car over. I was confused. Did mother understand what this job entailed? Surely, she did not or she never would have sent me there. Or would she?

I have no idea how mother found this job interview for me. I did not want to know. Mother and I did not speak for many weeks after this interview and neither of us ever brought it up again.

Chapter Eight:

The Calm Before the Storm

College was wonderful. I was fortunate to be awarded an academic scholarship to attend Arizona State University as well as a second scholarship for my dorm and books. As an emancipated seventeen -year-old, this was my biggest high school achievement. This allowed me to propel forward and attain the goals that helped me get through each day of my life at home.

I will be forever grateful to my high school counselor. I don't think he ever knew what was really going on in my home, but I believe he suspected there was something wrong. Those were the days before mandated reporting. What was there to report? I was fed and clothed. I was a good student. Only a trained and experienced professional would have noticed that the smile on my face covered the sadness inside.

I'm not sure what it was about me exactly that glared out at him, but something did. In the short time he was my counselor, he took me under his wing and guided me through the steps to be independent.

I entered my freshman year at the university with the twelve credits I had accumulated at the community college my senior year of high school. I led such an introverted and goal oriented lifestyle in high school that by the time I made it over to the university, I just let lose. I majored in Partying 101 during my first year at college.

I had a burning desire to be social and have fun. Having attended so many different high schools in three years, it had just been easier for me to be by myself. I had few friends in high school. I never spent long enough in each school to feel as though I fit in, like I did in New York.

During those high school years, I learned to squash the loneliness, just as I learned to squash my emotions, waiting for the day I would leave and go to college.

At Arizona State University, I had more friends and was happier than I'd ever been in my life. My grades were good, some A's, some B's, but they could've been better. I was finally balancing a social life with an academic life, and working as a waitress at a popular disco club. It felt like my life was finally my own. I could breathe for the first time.

I loved practicing judo and my volunteer work at the Center Against Sexual Assault. I dated a lot. I changed my major a few times to try to achieve the family expectation to be a lawyer.

In truth, I knew I didn't want to be a lawyer. I was fascinated with criminality, long before it became popular media. I had read about the Kitty Genovese Case in New York and although, I didn't know her, this case moved me deeply. Kitty was a nurse working the swing shift in New York City. She was stabbed in front of her apartment building walking home from work. She screamed out for help and no one came. People came to the window, but no one went downstairs to help or call the police. Then the unexpected happened, the assailant retuned and stabbed her repeatedly until he killed her. No one helped this nurse. I needed to understand why. This one case cemented my determination to work in the field I am in today; criminology with an emphasis on rage and violence.

I met with an advisor in the Criminology Department at the university. I had no way of knowing this meeting would change the course of my life.

My advisor, Dr. Gayle Shuman was caring, insightful, and engaging. He helped me to define my life's work and my passion. Dr. Shuman changed my life.

"I want to be an investigator," I told him. He responded with a smile reminding me that there were not many female investigators. "That's ok, I will be one of the first," I said returning the smile.

With Dr. Shuman's help, I put together a schedule of classes that would complement my major and help me advance as a more attractive job candidate. I focused on advancing my level of Spanish. I stayed fit with at least one athletic class a semester. I took business classes, communications classes, and any other class that would give me a better chance at achieving my goal to be an investigator.

When Vincent Bugliosi came to lecture about prosecuting Charles Manson, I was seated front row and center. By the time the lecture began, it was standing room only. Still to this day, I am appreciative that Mr. Bugliosi agreed to speak with me for a few minutes after the lecture ended so I could learn more about "Charlie". My dear advisor arranged this.

I was writing my undergrad paper about Charles Manson and had a few questions. Unlike others fascinated with his crime spree and Manson's charismatic ways, I had a different fascination. I was more focused on the hold that his charisma had and the depths it reached, grabbing ahold of intelligent, well educated people. Working on that project further reinforced my choice of career paths.

Dr. Shuman scheduled many volunteer opportunities for me as well. He explained these were to enhance my resume as well as provide an amazing opportunity to build a strong base of experience.

I volunteered at the Juvenile Detention Facility in Phoenix. He also arranged for me to volunteer ten hours a week at a halfway house for teens. I was busy and thriving.

The final opportunity he offered for my degree completion was an internship with the Office of the Attorney General of Arizona, Bruce Babbitt, in the Fraud Unit. I learned my basic investigation skills from the only female investigator in the office at that time. I followed her around not wanting to miss a moment of her brilliant, investigative skills.

Those trainings all served me well as I embarked on my career in criminology. I have thought about Dr. Gayle Shuman often in my life. From the first day, I met this retired FBI agent, turned university professor, he became my mentor, my friend, and my biggest supporter. We stayed close for almost five years after I graduated until I moved to Alaska.

He has since died, but his smiles of encouragement will forever live on in me. I'd like to think he is looking upon me and proud of the work I have done. Without him, I know I would not be doing the work I do today.

Yet, he too, knew more about the wounds in me than he had let on. During one of our last conversations, he shared what I believe was a mild version of his suspicions. He figured out that something was wrong in my home and I think he felt that my father did not respond to my mother's abuse. I denied the things he told me he saw. Now I realize he was right, I just wasn't ready to explore that part of my life at that time.

At the beginning of my junior year of college, I met my husband. I was intrigued with him from the start. I first saw Christopher when I pulled into a gas station to get gas and get my car checked under the hood.

I remember he was very busy. It was a late Saturday morning and the station was filled with students airing their tires to float down the Salt River for the afternoon. I was no different. After he filled the car with gas, I reminded him that he hadn't checked under the hood.

"Look, I'm really busy, can I get it next time?" I responded that he could not. He was not pleased with my answer.

Begrudgingly, he checked under the hood, "It looks fine, but you have the dirtiest transmission I've ever seen. It needs to be flushed," and he walked away.

The next day, I went to a mechanic savvy friend and he helped me flush my transmission. I returned to that same gas station a week later.

Again, I asked Christopher to look under the hood. "Again?" I just smiled. "I'm impressed!" He said. "Yup, I did it myself."

He wasn't as busy, so he stayed around and we talked a bit. He learned that I was a college student and a cocktail waitress at the most popular dance club in the university town, the Sun Devil Disco Club.

By this time, I had my own apartment. The scholarship still covered all my academics and books, but I paid for the rest of my living expenses.

There was going to be a big celebration at the Disco Club the following night. The event would be packed, as it always was, with lines out the door.

"Are you working the celebration?" he asked.

Shockingly I wasn't. I was actually going to have the night to enjoy the music, drinks, dance, play Pac Man, and sheer craziness without having to serve a drink!

I could see he didn't know what to say next, so I blurted out, "I'll meet you at the door at 9 and bring you in." I knew if he stood on line, he might not make it in.

For the next year, we dated. Christopher had been on a semester break from school when we met at the gas station. He had been a football player at Arizona State and left the team, needing to re-group. He had always wanted to be a teacher. He re-enrolled at the university and got a new job working with youth at a non-profit agency. He had found his 'nitch'. He loved his work and the community loved him even more.

I saw my parents occasionally during these years, sometimes at a restaurant for dinner or at their home for a home cooked meal. Mother was a wonderful cook.

These years were not turbulent for me. I had limited contact with my mother. My father would drive over and meet me for lunch once in a while. Our reduced contact was not an intentional plan. She was busy building her decorating business and I was busy with school, work, and my boyfriend. I definitely noticed my life was calmer and happier.

Chapter Nine:

The Wedding That Throws a Punch

I introduced Christopher to my parents. Dad thought he was a nice guy. Christopher and dad developed a relationship. Christopher frequently helped dad whenever there were heavy installations.

Mother seemed to hate him instantly and never failed to tell me how she felt. She had nothing but derogatory things to say about my boyfriend. At this point in my life, I was so independent I don't believe her opinion gave me much pause.

After about a year, Chris and I talked about getting married. When we told my parents, mother forced a smile and with an animated expression, she suggested we try living together first to see how that worked for us. That sounded like a good idea, so we did.

We didn't see mother and dad a great deal, but on the few occasions when we did, mother continued to make belittling comments to Chris.

"You are becoming a teacher. When are you going to grow up and get a real job?" Chris held his tongue until one day when he didn't.

After returning from a business trip to California, he let me know he found my mother too taxing and did not want to continue the relationship with me. I understood his decision. I called mother, furious.

She called Chris trying to make amends and apologize, but understandably, his mind was made up. I moved out.

I was twenty years old and had just graduated a semester early from college. Everywhere I went in Phoenix reminded me of my broken relationship and I felt sad. I needed to get out of Arizona.

I had a cousin who was living in San Francisco. He and his wife graciously invited me to stay with them, find a job, and relocate to California. I packed my car and in two days drove from Phoenix to San Francisco.

I tried my best to move forward, but I missed Chris. We didn't have cell phones then. When I left, he'd asked me not to call the number that used to be our landline, so I did not. I went on job interviews, met a few older men who offered to take me to dinner in Sausalito or go sailing in the Bay.

After six weeks, I felt joyless. I kept telling myself I should feel excited and embrace this new adventure. There were amazing possibilities ahead for me. I was scheduled for an interview with a prominent San Francisco Attorney who did criminal defense work and was nationally known. In addition, I submitted an application to Hughes Air West Airlines, on a whim.

I still loved criminology, but I was losing my fire. My parents checked in on me a few times a week. I visited some old family friends, but nothing I did seemed to help. I just wasn't happy.

My cousin and his wife left for a one-week vacation to Mexico. I was sitting alone in their beautiful house and I picked up the phone and called Chris. It felt strange dialing my old telephone number. He wasn't home.

I left a voice message, "Hey Chris, this is Sue. I just wanted you to know I was thinking about you. I won't call you again, but I just wanted you to know I am missing you. You don't have to call me back, but if you do, I would like that." I didn't expect him to call me back, but secretly I'd hoped he would. An hour later, he did.

He said he was missing me something awful and had rethought his decision. If I would just come home, he wanted us to continue where we had left off. I was elated and knew returning home was what I wanted to do. I loved him and wanted a family with him. Family was first and career second, became my new mantra.

The next morning, I left a note for my vacationing cousins, along with a plant, and told them of my change in plans. Then I began the long return to Phoenix in a brutal rainstorm that gained extra momentum in Santa Barbara. I couldn't even see the front of my car. It took me two extra days to get to Phoenix.

I went straight to my old house, excited to walk back into the life I had left. I did not tell my parents I was returning to Arizona. It felt awkward at first, something was wrong, but I figured it was because we were on new ground following our separation. We had a romantic night releasing all that had built up in these past six weeks.

The next day, again, the next day he told me he was having second thoughts about us getting back together due to my mother. I was heartbroken. "I just gave up a job interview with a prominent attorney and drove through a storm to get back to you. Now you don't know."

With disappointment, I left what was once again my old house, got a newspaper, and started looking in the Rental Section of the newspaper.

I had followed what my heart wanted. Even as I walked out, that had not changed. I found a townhouse right away. I had always been frugal with my money and had enough saved up for the deposit and first month's rent. I bought a bed and some cheap furniture then placed an ad in the newspaper for a roommate.

The next day, I went downtown, returning to find work with my former employer. During my last year in college, I had been a cocktail waitress at a popular five-star hotel and made incredible tips.

"May I have my old job back?" I asked my old boss. "You've graduated now, don't you want to work in your field?" was his response. "No, coming back here feels right for me for now." I had a need to embrace the familiar. I was not in the frame of mind to look for a job in my field until I cleared my head and found a routine, a new normal, and a sense of balance.

My funds were dwindling and I needed money. I couldn't wait months to get a job and a first paycheck. My boss only had a part time cocktail position available, so I supplemented that by working part time at the hotel's front desk as well.

Two weeks after I had returned, Chris came by my new townhouse. It was his birthday. I hadn't seen him since the first few days of my return. I missed him. We spent the weekend together. Little did we know, that night, we created the gift of a lifetime.

Over the next few weeks, we got together, without pressure or expectations. I remained in my own house, reconnected with old friends, and started dating casually.

I didn't trust us anymore, and wasn't up for any more roller coaster rides. Deep inside, I still loved him. Over dinner, one night, he said, "Susan I love you. I've been scared about your mother. I want to marry you." I wasn't expecting that and felt torn. I loved him, but my heart had been doing flips for over four months. "Let's take some time so I can show you that I mean it," he suggested. For the next two months, I kept my own place as we rebuilt our relationship. We even talked about getting married at the end of May.

About a week into our private engagement, I noticed I wasn't feeling very well. Anything with a tomato base or coffee made me violently ill. I had never experienced that before, I had always loved coffee.

Soon after I had returned to Phoenix, I also returned to my volunteer position with Planned Parenthood. I told my friend, the Director of the clinic, how I was feeling. She suggested I take a pregnancy test.

"That's ridiculous," I responded. "I just had my period, so I can't be pregnant." "Is it lighter than usual?" she inquired. Actually, it was. The pee test came back negative. "Let's try a Bi-Cep G Blood Test. I think you might be pregnant." She led me to an exam room for a blood test.

I was in shock. I had been so responsible using my new form of birth control, the diaphragm, except for the night of Chris's birthday. The test came back positive. I always wanted lots of children so I was happy, but I was scared that I wasn't ready.

I was twenty years old. I had a Bachelor of Science Degree, I had just landed a new job in the criminology field a week before, and I had saved $5,000 that I could cash it out if I needed it. That was a good chunk of change for a 20- year old in the late 1970's. "Maybe I was more -ready than I realized," I told myself.

That night I told Chris. I trailed it with a disclaimer that he did not have to feel pressured to marry me. I had a job making good money. I had just accepted a well-paying job. My pay was strong. I had a place to live. I could make it on my own.

I kept telling him, "You are under no pressure." He looked at me shocked. "I still want to get married, no disclaimer needed. Going for a run, be back in an hour."

I wasn't sure what to make of it, so I tried not to over analyze it. He returned an hour later. He kissed me and said, "I'm excited."

"How about we postpone getting married until after the baby is born, that way I'll be sure you don't feel you are under any pressure," I suggested following him into the bedroom after his run.

"Absolutely not. Let's go tell your parents and get that part over with."

We met them at a French bistro. I wasn't hungry, neither were they after they heard the news.

"How could you do this to me? What were you thinking?" mother was screaming in the restaurant.

Dad told her to sit in her chair and calm down. I looked directly at her.

"You know mother, I wasn't thinking about you at all when we made this baby." I got up to leave. "Come on Chris, let's go. Dad asked everyone to calm down and asked us to take our seats.

"What we are concerned about," he began, "Marriage is hard enough without children. When you bring children into the mix so quickly, it puts more strain on a new marriage. That's all. I'm happy for you both. Congratulations," and he hugged both of us.

"Well, I guess that doesn't leave much time to plan a wedding. I'll get on it tomorrow," was mother's response.

"That's ok mother, we are getting married by a justice of the peace."

"Absolutely not. I am calling the Camelback Inn and you will walk over the bridge on the pond in a wedding gown. I have planned this for a long time. I will have it all figured out tomorrow. Now let's everyone eat." I wasn't hungry.

The next day, as promised, mother called me. The Camelback Inn had a cancellation and we could hold the wedding in the middle of June. "It is amazing that I can pull this off so quickly," she said. "We have a lot to do. I will get started with the invitations. We will get them on a rushed basis. I want to get them mailed within the next few days."

"Wow, that's kind of quick," I responded bringing back memories of my sweet sixteen party. "I don't even have a list of people to invite yet."

The truth was we didn't have many people to invite. Many of our friends had graduated and were relocating to other states for their first job experience.

"You don't have to think that hard. Only eight people," mother said.

"I don't understand," I said confused. "What do you mean eight people?"

"Well, you and Chris are two. We have room for his side to invite eight more. I have compiled a list of ninety people from our side. We cannot afford more than one hundred people total. So, it shouldn't be that hard to come up with eight names," she announced with a hint of sarcasm.

Without taking a pause, she continued, "We need to get you a wedding dress. You are so tiny, you shouldn't be showing much by then."

I was still stuck on the eight people, and she was pushing this conversation forward. "Mother, let me get this straight. You have a list of ninety people and we can only invite eight people? Chris's family is bigger than that. I am going to need to get back to you." And I hung up.

The phone kept ringing and ringing after that. I would not pick up. There was no caller ID. I can only assume that the continuation of ringing could be from no one other than mother.

When Chris came home, I told him about the conversation. He suggested we go down to the White Mountains in Arizona and get married at the fork of the river by a justice of the peace.

We did just that. It was beautiful, unpretentious, and tranquil.

Putting her plans for our wedding gala on the shelf, mother was excited to greet us with yet another idea, the unconventional wedding reception she was organizing for us. She gave us the date. She insisted it was already planned. All we had to do was show up. The party was two weeks away.

Honestly, we were all dreading it. Mother still stuck to her "only eight guests for Chris rule," even though this celebration was now going to take place in my parent's lovely two acre backyard.

Years earlier, they had landscaped their entire one- acre parcel with an hour -glass shaped pool, an over-sized gazebo, and lovely brick paths for guests to roam and look at the foliage, dad's pride and joy.

Neither of us was looking forward to this event. I decided one way to make the celebration a bit more special was to fly Chris's mother to Arizona to join us for this joyous occasion. I wanted to surprise my new husband. I loved his family. They welcomed me as one of their own, the family I'd always wanted. I felt blessed to be part of them.

My parents and Chris's mother had never met. Initially, all were gracious at the beginning of the party, shaking hands and making small talk. We only invited four from our allotment of eight guests. Chris's sister and brother-in law were living in Arizona at the time, so they came. We also included an old family friend who had recently relocated near us. Chris's mother knew him. This way his mother had people to mingle with at our reception.

About halfway through the celebration, and after the buffet, Chris and I heard our mothers screaming at each other. We were by the pool about thirty- yards away. At first, we were not sure we actually comprehended what was being said. It seemed almost surreal.

"He isn't good enough for her!" mother was screaming. "You need to stop choking that girl and cut those apron strings!" Chris's mother responded.

We are not sure who pushed or hit first, but there it was. My mother and mother-in-law were shoving and screaming at each other in front of the guests.

We ran to them. Mother was fiery with rage. Dad tried to take mother inside the house. She wouldn't go. When that didn't work, he told the band's leader to start playing music. Dad was trying desperately to de-escalate this humiliating altercation at the celebration of his daughter's marriage.

We grabbed Chris's mother and headed to the car. We never ate the wedding cake or said our goodbyes or thank you to our guests. We drove to our apartment in silence.

Once we were at our apartment, Chris's mother asked if we minded if she returned home to her family, the next day, three days earlier than was scheduled.

We didn't speak to my mother again until a week before the baby was born, six months later.

Chapter Ten:

Happy New Baby!
Don't Call Me Again!

When I became pregnant with our second child, I was overjoyed. Our two children would be two years apart. Getting pregnant was never difficult for me, but this pregnancy was actually a lot tougher than the first. I was 112 pounds when I became pregnant and dropped to 97 pounds for the first few months.

Everything made me throw up, even sips of water. I had made multiple trips to the emergency room for IV hydration. My fatigue was so overwhelming; there were days, I could barely get off the couch.

I had resigned from my full-time job working investigations and as my energy returned, I took occasional substitute-teaching positions just to get some extra money. I had decided I wanted to re-group professionally and focus on getting a teaching certificate. Spending long periods of time on the couch also allowed me time to complete two certified credentials in the field of "Severely Emotionally Disturbed" and "Learning Disabilities". I had reasoned that if I could make a difference in the lives of young people, maybe that would keep them from walking down the path into the justice system. It was a deep desire I had once I had children.

Mother and Dad were a bit more involved with us now that they had a granddaughter and were about to have two. Dad adored his granddaughter. He found many reasons to stop by and see "his two favorite girls" as he called us. Sometimes he would bring his granddaughter a Happy Meal or other little treats. She loved her Poppy.

She also loved to swim. We started mother-baby swim classes twice a week, when she was six months old. On the weekends, I tried to set aside time to take her swimming at mother and dad's house while Chris was at work. Between going to school and working late shifts, he wasn't around in the evenings or much on weekends.

As I started feeling better and my appetite improved, dad would BBQ. It seemed like the only food I could keep down for the first five months was pie and ice cream. Not a bad choice! My husband would join us for an occasional Sunday BBQ if his schedule allowed.

One day, early in this second pregnancy, I was walking through a drug store with my mother and my daughter. My daughter was an active one and a half- year old, so having a second set of hands was truly appreciated. I started to faint and grabbed the shopping cart.

Mother immediately got me to the car, buckled in our toddler, and actually drove my car to her house, something she never did. After a few glasses of cool water, that I was able to keep down, I started to feel better. We laid my daughter down for a nap and I rested on the couch.

Mother was worried. I understood that, so I promised her I would call my doctor. I was going to see him in a few days anyway. We stayed a few hours and mother cooked dinner. I should have skipped dinner.

After dinner, Mother started to rant, "What is wrong with you? Don't you see this pregnancy is not meant to be? You need to start considering getting an abortion. You should not have this baby."

My only response to her was, "Not now mother."

Once I felt better, I drove to our home, an hour away. I told Chris about my mother's comment. He asked me what I thought about mother's comment to have an abortion. I acknowledged she was right about the difficulty I was having with this pregnancy, but I really wanted this baby. Deep down I had a feeling this baby was going to be fine and anything beyond that, I could handle. I had listened to mother's spewing, as she liked to call it, all of my life. Like most of mother's other episodes, I eventually pushed this one away.

My obstetrician felt I was high risk due to my chronic nausea and extreme weight loss, so he saw me bi-weekly for the first two trimesters of this pregnancy. I told him about the conversation with my mother. He was honest with me, and explained there were no guarantees. I already knew this. He asked if I wanted him to do an amniocentesis to check for abnormalities. I declined. The ultra sound machines were rather new then but he had me on them frequently. Each time, the report came back that our baby looks fine.

My doctor asked if we wanted to know the sex. "Of course!" At that time, the doctor shared that we were having a boy. We didn't have a preference, girl or boy; our wish was genuinely for a healthy baby.

For me, the last trimester was even more difficult. The baby dropped and stayed low almost the entire last trimester. It even made waddling difficult. I saw my doctor weekly for most of the last trimester. The doctor reassured me the baby seemed healthy.

Delivery day didn't come fast enough for my body. I had a scheduled C-Section at the end of March. I arrived at the hospital ready to greet our new baby into the world and into our family. Honestly, I was happy not to be pregnant any more.

The delivery was definitely eventful. Our beautiful baby girl was born with auburn red hair and a healthy cry. We laughed about technology and were thrilled to have two little girls. I was awake to share in that joy. "Our little girl was healthy," was the last thing I remember hearing.

I started to go into some distress as they were closing the C-Section. The anesthesia had started to wear off and I was put back under quickly. After the delivery, I was in recovery for a short time then taken to my room where I able to hold my baby. What a joy it was to be greeted by this little cherub.

A few hours after I had returned to my room, the doctor, who had now delivered both my daughters, paid us a visit. I adored him, so did Chris.

Our doctor walked into my room looking rather grim.

"What's wrong?" I asked immediately fearful that one of the baby's tests came back with a concerning result. "I need to talk to you both about something," he began. He was noticeably uncomfortable.

"Ok," we both said in unison. We were alarmed. "What is it?" I asked urgently, bracing myself for the bad news.

"Your baby is fine," he began. "All of her tests are back. Her APGAR scores are strong." He paused, looking uncomfortable. "I have something else to talk to you about. I have enjoyed having you as my patient for several years now and I have enjoyed getting to know Chris, but I will only continue to be your doctor through your six- week checkup. I will not be able to keep you on as a patient, should you decide to have a third baby."

I wasn't sure what to think. We had not even spoken about a third child since this pregnancy had been so difficult on me. I couldn't imagine why he would tell us this so soon after the delivery of our baby.

He repeated, "I will continue to care for you for the remainder of this birth and recovery for the next six weeks. Then I am going to have to let you go as patients."

I loved my doctor so I naively asked, "Why? Are you closing your practice?" That was the only reason I could fathom that he would drop us as patients.

"No, that is not the reason. My staff and I have been receiving an inordinate amount of telephone calls from your mother, often several times a day." "Oh, no," I gasped. I was devastated.

He continued, "She threatens our staff accusing us of not taking proper care of you. Earlier on, she insisted I encourage you to pursue discontinuing the pregnancy. She sounds like she is out of control. We are at the point now, we just hang up on her." I looked over and saw my husband looking down and shaking his head. I repositioned the precious daughter sleeping in my arms.

"On behalf of both of us," I began with my voice trembling, "I want to apologize for what my mother has put you and your staff through. I am mortified that she would do this. I am just so very, very sorry." He stood and shook Chris's hand. He came over toward my bed. I reached over and gave him a hug.

"I am appreciative to you and your staff for all the care you have given to our family. I understand. I just don't know what to say." He said he would see me at rounds the next day and left. We could tell he felt as badly as we did. The pain I felt in my belly was not from surgery. I felt like I had just been punched in the gut, yet again.

We didn't say anything about this to mother after our conversation with the doctor. For about a month following the birth of our second daughter, we intentionally did not see my parents much, we needed some distance. About two months after I brought the baby home, I asked mother about her calls to my doctor. She said the doctor was imagining everything. She insisted he was making all of it up. She told me those calls never happened.

I wish I could have seen her face. Unfortunately, we had that conversation over the telephone. After my six-week checkup, I never saw that doctor again. Once again, the feelings that she was trying to control my life were validated.

Chapter Eleven:

Moving Far Away

Once home with the new baby, I got into the routine of having both a toddler and a newborn. It definitely was an adjustment.

Our new baby was the most gentle, easygoing child any mother could have. She was easily entertained by her older sister who put on puppet shows for her, sang, danced, and just plain talked non-stop. Big sister helped me diaper the new baby and responded with glee when I would tell her it was bath time.

Once the girls were old enough to take baths together, they could play in the tub for hours. Sometimes, I would add more warm water and refresh the bubbles, so they could stay in longer.

When the new baby was four months old, she spiked a very high fever, was listless, and moaned frequently. Something was not right.

I brought her into our pediatrician's office. Dr. D was a father of eight children. This incredible man made himself available to us even as his own child was facing a terminal illness. Big sister loved to go see Dr. D and would run into his arms whenever it was time for a wellness visit. We felt fortunate to have a pediatrician we loved.

Unfortunately, Dr. D was not there when I came in with our sick baby.

There was a substitute doctor who said, "It looks like the baby has strep. She will need antibiotic." I had nursed her for only three months. She had been on formula for only a little over a month when she was diagnosed with strep. I couldn't understand how she could have contracted this.

Even after ten days of squirting liquid Amoxicillin into her tiny mouth with the syringe, she still was not getting any better. I started to notice her fontanel was protruding on the top of her head. Our pediatrician was back by then. I requested an emergency appointment and took her in. He immediately sent us over to the hospital where our little baby was scheduled for an emergency spinal tap.

As a parent, hearing her screams from the painful test was absolutely unbearable. I wanted to change places with my baby and let them stick the needles into me instead of her. The test results were requested on a rush basis and came back positive for spinal meningitis. The pediatrician was on his way over and would meet with us as our baby was admitted to PEDS ICU.

One of our neighbors was keeping our oldest daughter until we could get some semblance of what was going on. We had not spoken to mother or dad much since we became aware of mother calling my obstetrician. In those four months, Dad would call occasionally to see how the girls and I were doing. Sometimes we would meet him at McDonalds on a Saturday morning. I called my parents to let them know the diagnosis. That was a mistake.

The doctor explained that spinal meningitis could be bacterial and respond to an antibiotic, or viral, in which case the antibiotic may not be effective.

"The outcome is not good when a baby this young contracts spinal meningitis," he began. I had studied about spinal meningitis when completing my special education certifications. Frantically, I mentally retrieved the details and statistics associated with meningitis, but now they held a different relevance to me. This was my baby.

The doctor continued, "The odds are a twenty-five percent chance she will come out of this fine with just a few residuals, a twenty-five percent chance she would become deaf and /or blind, a twenty-five percent chance she would be developmentally disabled, and a twenty-five percent chance she would not make it at all." We were living a parent's nightmare. This could not be real. I kept hoping I would wake up from this nightmare.

"What do we do?" we asked.

"There are two different antibiotics we can use to treat meningitis on a baby this young. My recommendation is that we use both at the same time and hope that one of them works. I am concerned if we try one and it doesn't work, it might be too late to try the other." "Is there a down side to using both at the same time?" Chris asked. "Both medications will cause irritation to her veins, so I'd like to do two separate 'cut downs' above each of her ankles. We will feed one anti-biotic into one leg and the second antibiotic into the second leg. We are going to need to weigh both of her legs down with small sand bags so she doesn't kick the IV's out."

"Whatever you need to do," I said. I just wanted my baby to get well.

While they took the baby back to perform the cut down procedure, we walked out to the waiting area. My parents were waiting there. Mother's first response after hearing the news was again unforgettable and unforgiveable.

"This is all your fault you know. You went back to work and that babysitter of yours is a religious zealot. Who knows what goes on in that house? I told you while you when you were pregnant this baby was going to have problems." Then she walked away in disgust.

This is the first time I felt like I could punch my mother in the face. Instead, I walked away. At that instant I knew my mother could not be part of my children's lives in the way I'd hoped as a grandmother.

I needed to protect my girls. At that time, I don't believe I outwardly articulated that mother was incapable of being the normal grandmother as I hoped she would, but I knew that life for us was about to change once my baby was stabilized.

Our baby was taken back to her room after the cut-down procedures. That night, I went home to get our toddler settled and Chris stayed the night with the baby.

I couldn't sleep at all that night. I could not settle my brain. My thoughts were racing. As I closed my eyes, I would see those statistics about meningitis reappearing in my mind. I knew those percentages well. It was a struggle to keep them at bay. And deep within, my mother's words haunted me. Maybe she was right. Maybe my baby was fighting for her life because of me and my decision to go back to work.

I don't think I slept at all that night, but I did make an important decision, I would not abandon hope that she would survive, grow up, and have a good life.

The next morning, another friend kept our toddler and I went to spend the day in the hospital with my baby, while Chris went home for a quick shower and went to work. We needed the money desperately.

When I entered the hospital room, my baby suddenly appeared so small. They had her in a hospital bed with the sides pulled up. She was not in a crib. I took down one of the rails, climbed into the bed next to her, and lay beside her for the entire day. We kept that same schedule throughout the week.

Since she had the sand bags and blocks holding down both her legs, I was not able to hold her in my arms and rock her. Then it continued into week two. It was all I could do to hold myself together. I could not stop reliving my mother's words, did I create this situation for my baby?

Every day I read to my baby, sang to her, and told her stories that didn't make sense. I don't remember what they were about, I just wanted her to hear my voice and feel me lying next to her. Since the baby was in the PEDS ICU, the only visitors who were permitted direct contact with the baby were her parents.

Chris and I kept these daytime/night shifts up for almost four weeks. Our toddler changed caregivers each morning and evening. For one hour each evening, Chris and I would overlap our hospital time and catch up on the day, make decisions about the baby and converse, about her progress. We tried not to talk about the dreaded topic of bills and money. And when we were done talking, we held each other.

Since I was still substitute teaching and not back to a full-time job, my husband was our sole source of income. He had sick days but not a lot of them. His boss and colleagues were great support, allowing him to break away a few hours at a time.

Two weeks into the recovery, the baby seemed to be getting worse. The pediatrician came into the room with another doctor whom I did not know. They spoke medical jargon that fortunately or unfortunately I understood well from my prior training.

"She is becoming hydrocephalic," I heard one of them say. "We may need to do a shunt." I knew hydrocephalic meant water on the brain and immediately threw myself into the conversation.

"What about a brain tap without the shunt?" I asked. I thought it might have a faster result than a shunt. They turned toward me not realizing I'd understood the details of their consultation. "I have read about that procedure in my studies," I explained. "We don't have a doctor here in Arizona that can do that procedure" the other doctor responded. "Who can do this procedure?" I asked.

"I believe there is a doctor from San Diego who can do this procedure. The tools he uses are specialized for infants," my pediatrician responded.

I begged them to consult with him immediately. They tried to explain to me that they could not move the baby. It was too risky. I pleaded with them to call the specialist in San Diego. Then I asked if I could be part of that conversation. My wonderful pediatrician smiled, and said, "Of course." The two doctors and I sat in the room consulting via the telephone with the pediatric neurosurgeon from San Diego.

"We have the mother of the baby with us," Dr. D began. Our doctor proceeded to give the pediatric neuro-specialist the details of our daughter's health situation. When they were done, there was silence on the other end of the phone.

"May I speak?" I asked. In unison, they gave some affirmation. I begged this specialist to save our baby. I told him I did not care about the cost. I will pay him back if it takes the rest of my life, just please consider doing this procedure on our baby. I found myself promising him and bargaining with him that if he would help my baby, I would make it my life's mission to help every young person I worked with for the rest of my life.

The phone was quiet for another moment. The San Diego Specialist asked additional questions of the Arizona doctors. I stayed quiet. All understood the baby could not be moved. The specialist would have to come to her.

The pediatric neurosurgeon was going to fly in at 7am the next morning to do the brain tap procedure in hopes of reducing the swelling in the baby's brain, rather than our doctor's inserting a shunt.

Once the procedure was over, our doctor and the hospital team would continue to treat and monitor her. I immediately called Chris to give him the update. My husband took the next few days off. Together we sat with our baby as she fought for her life. We alternated sleeping with her. Friends kept our toddler. Big sister was missing her mommy and daddy, but we knew she was fine.

The nightmare of those days blended together as we prayed, promising God anything and everything if our baby was spared. We spoke of many what-if scenarios. We knew that whatever happened to our baby; deaf, blind, or delayed, we just wanted her to make it.

As we rolled into almost four weeks of our baby's hospitalization, we needed to change up the schedule. We started bringing our toddler with us to the hospital for a few hours each afternoon as Chris and I changed shifts. Even though big sister wasn't allowed to see her baby, she loved that time. She would look at her baby sister through the glass window to her room and wave.

"Tell my baby I love her, mommy." She would say.

The nurses and the hospital became our extended family and friends. They allowed our toddler in a play area exclusive for siblings. They even gave her popsicles, and would visit with her. This allowed my husband and I a few extra minutes alone.

After forty-five days in the ICU, our baby was released. She was not deaf nor was she blind. She seemed to respond as any other six-month old would at the time. Since we did not authorize the shunt, her doctor continued to have concerns that there might be a buildup of fluid on her brain. "How will we know?" I inquired. He told me if there was additional buildup of fluid, her head would grow. It was as simple as that. I was petrified to bring her home. I never told anyone that, but I was.

After we brought her home and settled her in her crib, I went to my sewing basket and took out my tape measure. At this point, there was no family routine to return to. I found myself wanting to rock my baby in my arms all day and not put her down. I measured her head several times a day, just in case.

Shortly after bringing the baby home, Chris returned to working full time. My mother and father came over one afternoon while Chris was working. I shared my obsession about measuring my baby's head.

Mother said, "You have already made peace with handling whatever happens with this baby, so stop measuring her head or you will drive her crazy."

I appreciated my mother's insight. There were moments when mother was normally engaged. Those were moments that I treasured. I found myself asking myself once again if there was a chance we could have a more normalized relationship, simply because I wanted it to be so.

Our Saturday's with dad resumed, except we no longer met at MacDonald's. Instead dad came to our house. I was constantly worried about the baby being exposed to germs or not having a strong immune system.

In time, the baby grew stronger and stronger. The pediatrician felt confident that the worst was over. He suspected the most we would be dealing with could be delays.

"She might be a late bloomer," he would say. Each stage could come a little later or take a little longer to get through. He suggested loving patience with her. Patience, I could do. Loving her was easy.

I lived in a chronic state of fear until her first birthday. I had stopped measuring her head, but I didn't sleep well. I woke up several times each night to see if she was breathing.

For her first birthday, we decided to give her a grand celebration. Everyone we knew came. We gathered at a park, grilled hamburgers and hot dogs, and she had her own little chocolate cake. That was the first time I had felt peace in a very long time. I looked at my baby smiling in her high chair and I thought if I could rename her, I would call her Faith. She was perfect, no delays, and no residuals so far.

From pregnancy to her first birthday this baby taught me to believe. My life changed a little every day after that.

Shortly after her birthday, we were able to establish a more normalized routine. I worked part time and Chris worked two jobs. We opened up a food concession business at a Bingo Hall and used all those proceeds to pay off the enormous doctor bills that the insurance did not cover.

Less than a year later, with more incidents of mother stirring the pot, criticizing, and raging about everything she perceived we did wrong, I begged Chris to move.

"I just can't stay here anymore," I told him. He was as frustrated as I was, but he was not sure he could get a job transfer. He agreed to try.

He came home a few weeks later with two transfer options, Texas or Alaska. That was an easy decision for me, Alaska. I was ready for a new adventure and Alaska was far away. He agreed.

The agency flew both of us up to Anchorage. He interviewed with board members. They showed us around Anchorage and we fell in love with Alaska. How could we not? It was beautiful. But Alaska was also very expensive and offered fewer choices at the stores than we were used to in the lower 48 states.

The winters were going to take some getting used to, but I was ready to go! My bags were packed. We agreed to give Alaska a try for two years, then we would re-evaluate.

We returned to Phoenix, and Chris had less than thirty days until his start date in Alaska. Within that limited time, he also had to drive one of the cars to Seattle, to catch the ferry. He really only had three weeks to get ready. There were many parties and tearful goodbyes, as many in Phoenix loved him.

We put the house up for sale. I decided to sell the house myself. Once the house sold, the girls and I would fly up to meet him in Alaska.

He rented an apartment before we arrived and put everything in place. We would explore buying a house, once we were both up there together.

Telling my parents was difficult. I understood it would be hard for them when we moved so far away.

With the excitement of this new adventure, this fresh start, I felt like I could breathe again. The fact that it was far away was an added bonus for me.

Sharing the news with mother and dad did not go well. I'd expected tears. Dad didn't say much. Mother said enough. "You are moving to Alaska. This will be the last day you will see me. I will not help you pack. I do not want to see the children again. I am going to cease being their grandmother and cease being your mother as of today. Goodbye." She walked away.

Dad gave us all a hug and walked away with her. Chris left several weeks later. The house sold relatively quickly. The agency sent movers to pack up the house and car. I did not see my parents at all during that time.

Once all the furniture was taken, I stayed with a friend for about ten days while the furniture was shipped north. The day before I left, I called my parents to say good-bye.

It was finally the day I had been waiting for, moving to Alaska. I checked our luggage at the counter and got our boarding passes. We were upgraded to first class for the first flight. I had never flown first class before.

I said goodbye to my friend and walked towards security with one toddler in my arms and the other holding my hand.

As I looked up, I saw my parents standing in front of the security area. They were waiting to say good-bye. I burst into tears and hugged them both not wanting to let go and desperately wishing it was different.

Chapter Twelve:

The Affair That Never Happened

When the girls were seven and nine, I had this deep desire for another baby, maybe even two more.

True to form, I become pregnant with our third baby very quickly. It was not a difficult pregnancy. The biggest challenge was the incredible amount of weight I gained. I had only gained twenty pounds with each of the girls and lost the weight within a month of giving birth.

Getting back into my size 5 pants had never been difficult before. But this time, I was approaching sixty pounds of pregnancy weight. An early ultra sound revealed our baby was a boy. I just laughed saying "I'll believe it when I see him!"

They were right this time. Baby number three was a healthy 7.3 pound boy, 21 inches long, and with blonde hair. I now had my three "Neapolitans" as I called them, one with dark hair, another with auburn hair, and now one blonde. He was a consistently fussy baby, unless I carried him every moment of the day. I was thankful to the person who invented the Snuggly. It saved my sanity with this little guy.

We were well entrenched in the Anchorage community by that time. We had friends and a full life. I was happy. A few weeks after the birth of my son, Christopher was given an opportunity to work out of town for ten days. It had the promise of being lucrative. I told him to take the work. I'd be fine. He stayed for the delivery and for a few days after to make sure I was settled at home.

My mother offered to come up and spend a week with me right after he left. I always held out hope that one time we might have a normal mother-daughter relationship. Would that ever change?

I wanted just one visit without a full on explosion. I craved that, just one time. Even though I always told myself to be on guard, not to have expectations, I was privately hoping this time would be some good bonding time between us.

Mother arrived in the afternoon and slept in the girl's bedroom. The girls were excited to camp out in the family room while their grandmother was visiting. After unpacking, mother came into the living room where I was nursing my son. I invited her to grab a cup of coffee and sit with me.

With a mug of coffee in her hand, she sat across from me and casually said, "You know I almost didn't come on this trip."

"Oh, what happened?" I asked trying to sound nonchalant and praying this would not be another episode. I expected her to say there had been a problem with the house or with dad. Instead I was thrown for a loop when she told me that her doctor couldn't contain his feelings for her any longer.

According to mother, her doctor admitted he was physically attracted to her and to show her just how much, he invited mother to a remote lodge for a weekend fling. She begrudgingly told him that she would like to take him up on that offer, but she was obligated to come to Alaska and help her daughter with her new baby. I wasn't sure how to respond to that. Dad was home at the time.

I had many thoughts going through my head, "Does dad know?"

Then I spurted out, "You are married. He is my father. Why would you tell me something like this?"

She did not respond, she just looked at me. Momentarily, I was distracted with nursing the baby. I brought my attention back to the conversation we were apparently still having.

I told my mother she was always welcome to stay with me and enjoy the new baby and her granddaughters, but if she wanted to go home to take advantage of this offer, she could leave.

She responded, "No, he said it was a one-time weekend offer. It is no longer an option."

"Well, there you go," I responded and changed the subject.

Chapter Thirteen:

The Beginning of The End

Following my mother's visit after the birth of my son, I did not see her and dad again for year and a half. We spoke on the telephone, more with mother than dad. They always had an excuse why they didn't want to come up for a visit. This meant we would have to go to Arizona to visit them. It was expensive to fly with a family of five. Chris insisted we stay in a hotel and have a rental car so we could remove ourselves once her rage started. Those trips just never happened.

It was a constant struggle for me modulating the relationship I had with my parents. Dad didn't talk much and mother would flip back and forth so much, it was exhausting. There was always a fine line for me, protecting my children from her, yet desperately wanting them to know and be close with their grandparents. I have always held a core belief that a child should honor and respect their parents and grandparents.

I worried what kind of example this was setting for my children. How could I ever explain to them these rollercoaster rides? When mom was good with them, she was fun and happy. I never knew if that side of her would last an hour or a day, but without fail there were always episodes of rage at some point. When she was triggered and started spewing, there was absolutely no escalation time. The psychotic rage just came on so fast over something inconsequential and rocked me to the deepest depths of my core. I would ask, "What just happened?" Early on, I would ruminate about what triggered her. There was not usually an answer to that.

I so desperately wanted it to be different. A heavy heart stayed with me always in respect to my parents. I still loved them, but felt a pull inside every time I thought of them. I remained dutiful for most of the first fifteen years I was in Alaska.

Since I worked long hours during the week, I called every Saturday late in the afternoon, to share the week's happenings, and to inquire about how they were. If that time didn't work for them, I would call back on Sunday, always in the late morning. It was my time to sleep in. After a cup of coffee and making everyone breakfast, I would call. I tried to limit our conversations to an hour. And they always ended the same way, "OK mom, great chatting, I'll let you go, I have to get the kids going for the day." She insisted that I couldn't let her go, she would let me go from the conversation. I always agreed, told her and dad I loved them and promised to talk again in a week.

If dad answered the phone, we always went through the same three questions. "How are you Susie babe?" "Kids good?" "When will you be coming down to Arizona so we can see you?"

Every time I asked dad how he was doing or suggest he come up for a visit, he always responded with the same phrase, "Let me give you to your mother." I asked mother about dad's lack of engagement.

"He's fine," she insisted. I believed her. I thought they were busy enjoying their lives; going to concerts or out to dinner. They were considering closing their business. There had been an increase in the number of big box stores in their area and they couldn't compete with their prices.

They didn't seem to have many friends. When I would inquire about this, mother would tell me people had a hard time warming up to dad. She said people called him a blow heart and a braggart, so they didn't keep friends long. Dad always had a close extended family. I asked him whenever we spoke if he was in touch with them. He would just say, not in a while without any more details. It took me two decades to learn that she forbad him to speak to them. I am still heavy hearted about this.

When our baby boy was a year and a half old, and the girls were eight and ten years old, I was diagnosed with thyroid cancer and was told I would need surgery.

A cancer diagnosis was overwhelming to me, especially having three young children. I was advised that the biggest risk I would have was losing my voice permanently. I stayed up late at night, after I put the children to bed taping some of their favorite stories, so if they couldn't hear my voice first hand, they would always have the tapes. I vowed to myself that we would all learn sign language and we would come out fine on the other end.

My mind didn't seem to rest during the two weeks I waited for surgery. Late at night was always the worst, when I could be quiet with my thoughts. There were a multitude of them racing through my mind; one of which was wishing I had a mother I could call who could assure me everything would be ok. Mother was not that kind of a parent. I never called her mom. I always called her mother. One night, listening to my heart and not my head, I called mother and asked if she could come to Alaska to help me.

The surgery was scheduled for early on a Monday morning. Mother would fly in on a Saturday afternoon. Luckily, I was only scheduled to spend one night in the hospital.

The next two weeks were one of the most difficult times in my life. The surgeon, who had been highly recommended for this surgery, was going to be on vacation for two weeks. I elected to wait for his return, rather than have the surgery with a less experienced doctor.

During the wait for the doctor to return, everything felt fresher with the kids. Every moment was more vibrant. I felt a sense of urgency when I was with them. I never wanted each moment to end. I didn't want the children to fall asleep at night. The hardest part of the day was when everyone was sleeping and I was alone with my thoughts. I did not sleep very much during that time.

Sometimes, I just stood at their doors and watched them sleep. Then I would spend hours writing in my journals. I had three different journals, one for each of the children. There were many things I wanted them to know in case I didn't make it, which the doctor said was always a possibility. I used the precious darkness of the night to write, so I wouldn't miss a moment of togetherness with them during the day. The darkness of night gave me permission for my tears to flow. The light of day was filled with smiles that held back those tears.

Every night the same reoccurring thought came to me. It was not the possibility that I would be unable to speak, but the thought that the cancer had spread. It was unbearable for me to try to comprehend not living to see my children grow up.

I thought of all the things I would miss, their graduations, proms, weddings, and their children. It created such heaviness in my heart that some nights it left me struggling to breathe. My baby son, would never know me. I prayed for strength every night. Sometimes, I needed to pray for strength hour to hour.

As scheduled, mother flew in Saturday night, two days before the surgery. We all sat down to dinner. It was somber and only the kids were talking. They didn't know I had been diagnosed with cancer. They were excited to see their grandma. Chris, mother, and I did not speak about the potential side effects from this delicate surgery.

On Sunday, the day before the scheduled surgery, mother let me know that the timing for my surgery was a major inconvenience. She and dad had a family function to go to. My cousin was getting married in Las Vegas. She said she would have preferred for me to extend my surgery for another week so Dad did not have to attend the wedding alone. Dad went alone anyway. Mother insisted he needed her there for support.

There was nothing I could say. I just looked at her and again could not respond. For me, every moment was spent focusing on how to survive this cancer and be with my children. It was that simple, but that complicated. Cancer was also complicated on a social level. We think people will rally around us to help us through. Maybe some do, but I chose to keep the news of my cancer very contained within my small group. I noticed some of the other young mothers who were aware I had cancer, were hesitant to be around me. Perhaps I was a reminder of something awful that can happen to a young parent who had young children.

The day before the surgery, Chris and I took the kids to Chuck E. Cheese for an afternoon of air hockey, bowling, and pizza that tasted like cardboard. We had fun. The baby rode the rides and we all smiled at the Chuck E. Cheese Show. Mother preferred not to join us. She said Chuck E. Cheese was not her cup of tea.

I didn't sleep much the night before surgery. I cuddled with the children, reading them more stories than I usually did. I hugged mother goodnight and thanked her for coming. At 5am, the next morning, Chris took me to the hospital.

As the anesthesiologist was putting me under, he unknowingly asked me the wrong question, "Can you tell me about your children?"

I started to cry uncontrollably. All that I had held in for the previous two weeks came spilling out as I went under. Upon waking up, my friend who was also our family doctor was holding my hand. I remember she told me the doctor felt optimistic that he was able to get all of the cancer. She advised me not to talk, and I fell in and out of sleep.

The next thing I remember was one of the nurses saying, "Watch her neck," as they counted to three and moved me from the post op gurney to my hospital bed. I fell back to sleep. I was so exhausted, all I wanted to do was just sleep. Sometime that afternoon, I awoke with Chris holding my hand and calling my name. I remember hearing him, but it was like he was on the other side of a cloud of fog.

He annoyed me so much. He just kept calling my name. "What! Let me sleep," I answered in my grogginess. He smiled and I knew I still had my voice. That night turned out to be more difficult than was expected. I was nauseated from the anesthesia, which could have become an issue ripping my internal stiches.

Chris went home to see the kids for a few hours while my doctor-friend sat with me. She was not only my family doctor; she was an angel. She talked about everything and nothing. It was just so soothing to hear my dear friend's voice. She has since passed away. Still to this day, thinking of her brings a smile to my heart.

Later that evening, Chris came back and spent a few hours with me. Sometime after midnight, he went home for a few hours of sleep.

The next morning, after he took the baby to the sitter, and the girls to school, he returned to the hospital ready to take me home. Mother remained home to get ready for my arrival.

When the doctor came in he said he was not comfortable releasing me as planned, as he was still concerned about my nausea. He wanted to see how I progressed the remainder of the day. If my nausea subsided, I could be released later in the day. He said he had some other news to share. My first thought was that mother calling his office and harassing his staff. I reminded myself I had never given her the name of that surgeon, so I surmised it wasn't that.

Chris and I held hands as the doctor proceeded to share the results of the required pre-operative chest x-ray. The doctors found a sizeable spot on one of my lungs. They would do further exploration once I had a chance to heal from this surgery. "What are you thinking this could be?" I asked my surgeon. "Why don't we wait and see," he suggested, "rather than then get caught up speculating."

In my heart, I already knew. I had done a great deal of reading about thyroid cancer prior to this surgery. Since this was before computers and the internet, I did most of my research in books at the library. I had also requested my records from New York Children's Hospital where I had been for almost a month when I was about six months old. Mother had insisted the doctors perform exploratory surgery, wanting to find out why I had such a rapid weight loss and my failure to thrive. Instead, they did a series of x-rays that were calibrated too high for an infant. The long-term effects and levels of x-ray were not as understood back in the late 1950's. I was a textbook classic thyroid cancer as a result of excessive radiation as a child. It came to light exactly thirty years after the exposure which was also textbook classic.

By mid-afternoon, we were still unsure if I would be come home or remain in the hospital for another night. Chris brought mother to the hospital that afternoon for a visit. She bought me a darling, miniature stuffed seal from the gift shop. Mother had seen my seal collection in the house and was excited to add to it. I loved the seal. It is still a part of my collection today.

After Christopher took mother home, he picked the girls up from school and the baby up from the babysitter. He told the girls that mommy had her tonsils out and would either come home later that night or first thing the next morning. Mother assured my husband that she could handle the routine at the house, homework, dinner, and baths, so he returned to the hospital. The nausea subsided and I was released about 8:30 that night.

Once I walked in the door, I could immediately sense a chilly feel of the house. The girls didn't make eye contact with me. The baby was fussy. Chris grabbed him and I took the girls downstairs and tucked them into their beds. They asked about my tonsils and I assured them I was fine. I had a small bandage covering my throat. I kissed them and told them mommy needed to rest for a few days, and then I would be fine.

The girls told me grandma never stopped yelling all afternoon and evening. She kept hitting the baby because he wouldn't stop crying.

I explained to them that it was not OK for grandma to scream and hit. "She must have been really stressed," I said making up an excuse.

I told the girls mommy was home now and I would be taking care of them.

At that time, I was not aware that significant stress contributed to a borderline's behavior. I didn't even know she was a borderline at that moment, but I knew there was definite instability, mood dysregulation, and more, but I didn't explore this situation any further until a little later. My days were so filled with being a working, young mother and wife, I think I subconsciously squashed the journey to find out the truth about my mother because I wasn't ready to deal with all that would come with the realities and effects that would come later in my life with her. If I'd understood then, what I know now, I never would have asked for her to help me, even though I desperately needed my mother near me. I have no idea how I would have dealt with the depth of her personality disorder and how I would have walked that path with her then. It came to me later, when challenging as it was, I was better able to modulate the incredible sadness that would rock my soul.

The next morning, we settled into our daily routine. Chris took the baby to the babysitter, the girls to school, and he went to work. I slept in until mid-morning, still exhausted from the stress of this ordeal and two weeks without much sleep. I went downstairs to the kitchen and made myself a cup of coffee. Mother was taking a shower. I returned upstairs with my mug of coffee and crawled back into bed. I was starting to feel a bit more relaxed.

After her shower, mother saw my bedroom door was open and came upstairs. "You're up," she said in a bland tone. I apologized for sleeping so late. I told her I was just plain exhausted. I invited mother to grab a cup of coffee and come up and visit with me for a bit. I was going to share with her about the doctor's findings from the x-ray. I never got the chance.

She returned to my room without the coffee. The only way I can describe her face was contorted. "What's wrong?" I asked sitting up against the wall sensing something was very wrong.

She stood at the foot of my bed and screamed for twenty minutes non-stop. I know this because there was a digital clock on my nightstand.

In those twenty minutes, she told me she was tired of having such a loser for a daughter. As she raged on, the veins in her face started coming out, her fists clenched almost as much as her jaw. She was furious. "When are you going to get your shit together and stop being such a fuck-up? What a disappointment you are!"

I still remember the tears streaming down my face. Once again, I was totally blown away by another psychotic episode. Even after decades of dealing with her raging behavior, her words hurt me like a slap in the face, each and every time. This time it cut especially deep.

When she was done raging, she repeated what she always said after an explosive episode, "I'm done spewing now" and then she'd take a deep breath.

"Now, go pack your bag," I said with the tears still streaming down my face. I thought I was going to be sick. I could not believe the things she had just told me. "I'm better now," she responded straightening her hair.

"I need you to get out of my house, right now. Please go pack." I tried to stay calm. It was getting more difficult. Mother walked out of my bedroom, yelling once again, that her return ticket was not for a few more days.

I got out of bed, walked to my door and said, "Don't worry about that, we are going to get the ticket changed." Fortunately, we had a telephone in our bedroom. I called Chris at work and told him what happened. Then I called my doctor friend. I asked her to write a note to the airline requesting an emergency ticket exchange so mother could leave Alaska early. Then I locked my bedroom door. For the next ten years, I did not speak to my mother.

That shrilling and psychotic episode was one of the worst I had ever seen. It is an image that is still deeply entrenched in my brain and haunts me.

Thirty days after my cancer surgery, I was back to specialists taking more tests to determine whether the cancer had spread to my lungs.

It was determined it was not cancer. The scar on my lungs was from histoplasmosis, a virus I apparently developed when I was riding horses in the deserts in Arizona. I was cleared and for the first time in over a month, I felt calm and slept deeply.

Soon after mother left, I wrote her a letter telling her how sad I was. When I needed her the most, she let me down. At that time, I didn't know anything about borderlines. It wasn't talked about. I wish I had known, I think I would have handled things differently.

Mother responded to my letter. As she had done in the past, she insisted I fabricated the incident. She wrote that she was a sensational mother and had nothing to apologize for. Dad called me a few weeks later. I had a difficult conversation with him. I told him about mother's aggressive behaviors with the children and another raging episode with me. I tried to explain to dad that I couldn't subject the children to those psychotic behaviors. And quite frankly, I couldn't take then anymore. I explained that it was not a decision I had come to easily and I was still tortured by the thought of it.

Dad said he was struggling because mother insisted I was lying. I told dad I was worried about him and concerned for his safety. I told him several times during that conversation that he always had a place with us. He was most welcome anytime for as long as he liked. Mother was not. Dad told me he needed to live with the choices he made in his life. I said I understood. I told him I loved him and was only a phone call away. I stopped in a few times over those decades to check on them.

I could only stay a few minutes because the minute I would walk in, mother would start raging and shrilling.

Once I moved out of their home, mother had shifted her wrath, solely focusing on him. Dad stopped talking to everyone shortly after our phone conversation and he retreated into a kind of cocoon. He became mute. I wasn't sure if he processed anything said to him because he just didn't answer anyone. He had a sad and blank stare to his eyes. I would look right into them during one of my few stops to check on them, begging him to search deep in his soul and come back.

I thought that would be the last conversation I would ever have with my dad, until he called twenty-five years later. That beautiful voice I had not heard for decades said, "I think your mother is dying."

Chapter Fourteen:

Getting the Attention of Others

After my recovery from cancer, I did not speak with my mother or dad for ten years. I just couldn't understand mother's denial of her psychotic episodes. I could not expose my children to these behaviors. They had already been exposed to it once; there would not be a second time. In those ten years, Dad never called. I sent cards on birthdays and holidays.

Eleven years after I'd last seen mother, I received a call from her telling me things were starting to take a downward spiral. Dad was diagnosed with carcinoma on one of the lobes of his lungs. Mother had taken meticulous care of dad's medical needs in much the same manner she took care of mine before I had emancipated.

The surgery was scheduled on the first available date. Dad was not speaking at that time, so mother made all of the decisions and answered all of the questions asked by doctors and hospital staff. I believe that the staff thought dad had some kind of dementia and that was why he didn't speak.

I flew in on a Wednesday and returned home on a Sunday. I would have preferred to stay longer. I was in the process of getting divorced. Now being a single parent, I worked two jobs, and I just wasn't able to take more time off for dad's surgery unless there were complications.

Mother was furious that I could not stay to help with dad's postoperative recovery. She let me know I was on her shit list as she referred to it and would not speak to me or acknowledge my presence for the first two days I had returned to Arizona.

I spent most of those five days with my dad in his room in the ICU. He was having a hard time getting a handle on the pain and was extremely uncomfortable. I spoke with the nurses about increasing his medication since dad seemed to be in so much pain and seemed unable to communicate with the staff or with me using speech. His hospitalization was longer and his recuperation was slower than anticipated. His medical team recommended that dad recover in a rehabilitative nursing home facility. Mother would not hear of it.

On the third day after dad's surgery I left dad's room at the hospital and went down to the lobby for a cup of coffee. I could hear my mother screaming. Mother was furious that I could not stay to help her with dad for a few weeks post -surgery. She started yelling again about her damn kid.

I joined in the conversation, trying to explain the benefits of dad going to a nursing home for just a few weeks so he could get stronger. I told her it would be easier for her if he went to the nursing home.

Defensively, I continued to explain to the social worker why I couldn't remain in Arizona. I tried to get her to understand as much as I wanted to stay, I had jobs, kids, and I could not. I promised to return as soon as I could. Mother's fury would not be controlled and she continued to rage on. This was the second time she got the attention of others.

I recalled that decades earlier, dad had told me about mother's first public display of rage. He was still speaking at that time and had shared about an episode at a fund raiser dinner that he and mother had attended. He had waved at a female judge he saw across the room, having served as a juror in her court the week before.

He said in a split second, mother went into a rage yelling, "Are you fucking that bitch?" Dad was humiliated and said nothing. They were escorted out of the event. That was one of the few times dad had spoken ill of mother.

This time, during dad's hospitalization, mother's performance was in front of a myriad of nurses, social workers, and other hospital staff. She was the center of attention. I was escorted into a separate conference room and asked a series of questions by social workers. Mother was outside the door yelling at me to shut my mouth and let her answer the questions about dad. "You (social workers) never bring anything good to a situation," she raged.

Watching her through the glass in the door, I became quiet. Looking straight at me she continued, "What happens in our house, stays in our house." I just looked down, once again feeling her intense presence wrapping around me. I thought I had broken her emotional hold over me in the last ten years, but I was wrong.

Ultimately, mother refused to permit dad to go to a nursing home for the care he needed for recuperation. She brought him home and nursed him herself. Doctors prescribed post-operative pain medications and another drug for dementia. Mother told me she never gave dad the medication for dementia.

When I would call to check on dad, I never knew what my mother's demeanor would be. I was greeted with either a tongue lashing about what an awful daughter I was, or about how slowly dad was healing. Speaking with dad was not an option. I asked her to put the phone to his ear so I could tell him I loved him. I am not sure if she ever did that. She'd wait a minute or so after she and I had finished talking and then she would hang up.

Inwardly, I felt chronic guilt about my dad. As a single mother, raising three children on my own, I could barely afford the cost of ongoing trips from Alaska to Arizona, airfare, hotels, meals, and car rentals. Additionally, my job did not afford me a lot of leave time.

I offered to come to Arizona for our two-week winter break. Her response was, "I have it under control. I don't need you now." Secretly, I was glad. It was a relief both emotionally and financially.

I never viewed returning to Arizona as going home. Every single trip to Arizona delivered volatile, psychotic screaming. As she got older, she was getting worse.

Nine months after dad's surgery, I invited mother and dad to come up to celebrate Thanksgiving with us. It would be dad's third trip to Alaska. It had been over twenty-five years since dad had visited us.

Mother's response was that the trip was conditional. She explained the itinerary had to include a flight with three stops. I explained they could take a three-hour flight to Seattle, with a layover there. Then there was another three-hour flight from Seattle directly to Anchorage. Mother's response was that she would not bring dad on this trip unless there were three stops. To this day, I do not understand why she demanded three stops.

To appease her, I was considering another option; Phoenix to Portland, Portland to Seattle, and then Seattle to Anchorage. That seemed more arduous to me, but those were the conditions she required.

I never had to give any further thought to flights with three stops. Her final condition was a deal breaker. She insisted that dad be examined by a competent doctor as soon as he landed, one who could evaluate dad's condition immediately after travel. She wanted the doctor's name and telephone number ahead of time. "I'll get back to you, mother." I never did.

Chapter Fifteen:

Selling the Family Home

Almost ten years after dad recuperated from surgery, mother decided to sell their family home. It was a lovely, spacious three- bedroom ranch home with large bedrooms, a lovely kitchen, and an informal dining room-great room combination; perfect for entertaining or family dinners. Sadly, neither occurred with much frequency.

There was even a large study for dad and his books. The best feature of all was the land that came with the house. Mother and dad had bought the house and enjoyed selecting their flooring, tile, and all the interior enhancements of buying a new home. They added a large swimming pool with a diving board when they purchased their home.

Within the first year, dad built a lovely gazebo he designed. It included a large BBQ and sitting area. That allowed us an opportunity to visit with him when he grilled. He loved to BBQ and had spent a great deal of time under that gazebo before he retreated inward.

A few years after they moved into their new home, they also added a mother-in-law apartment to the back of the property. It was primarily used to store mother and dad's materials for the new business they had opened. I had only lived in this house for less than two years. It was a lovely house, but to me, home was the house we had sold in New York and where I lived until I was fourteen years old.

At the time of selling the family home, Dad was becoming less and less involved with the upkeep of the property. When mother called, she told me dad still did some light raking and cleaning out of the pool with a large net. That was it. He spent the majority of the day in his office, reading the hundreds of history and biography books he had collected over the years.

Every night Dad went to bed directly after dinner. He awoke early in the morning. I remember that this had always been his favorite time of the day. He loved to sit outside with a cup of coffee and watch the birds, and just listen to the sounds of the desert in the morning. I imagine that must have been a very lonely time for mother. She was more of a night person. Dad was already in bed by seven o'clock every night.

Several decades of the Arizona sun and desert had taken a toll on their house and it was in dire need of repairs. Their roof was leaking and all of the flooring needed to be replaced. Mother tried to keep the house clean. She had always been a spotless housekeeper or she hired someone to do the cleaning. Now, mold was growing in the showers and the tub. Most of the plumbing was leaking. It was obvious the house needed some serious attention.

Mother and I were speaking on a sporadic basis at this point. After dad's surgery, I called weekly just to check in with them, or I should say with mother. Dad no longer spoke on the telephone.

During one of our conversations, mother shared how arduous a task it was to pack up the home they had lived in for thirty years. She was right. Many things had accumulated over the years and had not been discarded. I appreciated the emotional toll this was going to be on mother, but she insisted she was ready and desperately wanted to move out of this house.

I offered to come to Arizona to help with the packing for a few weeks in early August, before I returned to school for the new school term. At that point I was running a program for severely high risk students as well as teaching college. Finally, I was getting on my feet and was able to afford the costs for me to travel to Arizona alone. Staying in their home was not an option for me. Hotel and car rental rates in August were greatly reduced. That would be helpful.

I asked mother if we could spend some time going through photo albums one evening while we were packing. I didn't have any pictures of my childhood or milestones of my life. I thought that could be a nice bonding time for us. Mother insisted she needed my help packing in September. I tried to explain to her I had to start school the end of August. I was not able to take two weeks off so early in the school year unless it was an emergency.

I came up with an alternative. I offered to go through the house in August, throw away, donate, or box things ahead of time. I tried to convince mother that the boxes could remain in the house until

September. At least we would be able to par down. She refused my help and said she would look elsewhere. She was disappointed once again she could not count on me when she needed me.

I don't know what ever happened to any photos that were taken of my childhood. I'm not aware of any photos taken of the milestones of my life (birthdays, first days of school, graduation, my wedding reception). To this day, I have very few.

I was frustrated and did not speak to mother again for a month and a half, until end the of September. She called frantic that dad was running in front of the house yelling "No! No!" as liquidators were loading their trucks full of the things mom had sold to them. I was not there to witness this on moving day. There was nothing I could do.

Mother had decided they would move to an apartment in Sun City. It was an independent apartment complex connected to a nursing home. Mother said she wanted to prepare for the day dad would need progressive care so it was close by. I was sad for them and the trajectory of their final years with no friends or no family around them.

Mother moved most of their bedroom furniture and re-created their new bedroom the same way as their old one, so dad could feel familiarity in their new apartment. She also had many of his books moved and placed on shelves in a half office space off the living room. Their new kitchen was galley style, barely big enough to open both the refrigerator and stove at the same time. This wasn't much of an issue since their new living community provided three meals a day.

After they were settled in their new apartment, mother called me to give me their new land line telephone number. I inquired how dad was acclimating to the new apartment. I knew he would miss the tranquility and richness nature provided him in their lovely backyard. Dad always loved the birds and the animals. Mother told me that he was the same and she had me to thank for dad not speaking any more.

"Your father has been miserable since the day you moved away. He's never been the same since. I cannot forgive you for that."

In my head, I knew she was right. I did leave Arizona. I did move far, far away to Alaska. The defensive voice in my head tried to reassure myself that I had invited them to visit often in the beginning. In all of the thirty-plus years we have lived in Alaska, she visited three times and dad came twice. I felt badly about not seeing dad more, in the beginning.

For a family of five, airline tickets, hotel, a car, and food were expensive. This was not a trip we could afford easily or often. School schedules only allowed us to travel during the most expensive times of the year. I reminded myself over and over again as if I needed constant reassurance.

Over the twenty-two years we were married, our family took few vacations. When we did, we wanted to relax and create memories for our family. As much as we wanted our children to know their grandparents, we knew with certainty that every visit was sure to include at least one or two episodes with mother's psychotic raging.

We walked on eggshells trying to avoid topics that might set her off. Yet, we never knew what those were exactly. Deep inside, her comment got to me. There was a piece of me that believed she was right. Was I the reason my father stopped talking? I wish we could have been like other families, but I knew my marriage wouldn't have lasted if we stayed in Arizona and I believed I would lose my mind if I was subjected to those psychotic rages on a steady basis.

I thought back to all of our special Saturdays that Dad, the girls, and I had before our move. I thought of the many afternoons when dad would drop in just because he was in the area. I loved those times. He loved his granddaughters and they adored him.

I believe dad would have adored the Alaska wilderness, if only I could have had the opportunity to share that with him. It would have been so much easier for my parents to come to Alaska than for the five of us to fly to Arizona with any regularity. I tried to hide the resentment I felt about that.

They did fly up to see us about a year after we moved to Alaska. Mother and dad flew up and stayed for only two days. A bizarre thing happened; they insisted they had to fly to Los Angeles because someone in my family had a car that had broken down on the highway and therefore they could not stay. I never did understand why this could not have been handled by a towing company. I was crushed and within hours they were gone.

They returned three years later. During that trip, our yellow lab gave birth to nine puppies. Dad was delighted. He always loved dogs.

I considered that to be a very good trip. The puppies were at the stage they were leaving their mother and exploring the house. It was a two- story house and the puppies were all over the place. The brave one's navigated the double set of stairs with delight.

We laughed a lot during that trip. One day, dad put his foot in one of his slippers only to find a warm, squishy, dark colored gift inside left by one of the puppies. We laughed until our stomachs hurt and kept laughing for days about that. Dad was a good sport, he would just roll his eyes, especially when we threw the slippers away and bought him a new pair. That was the last time dad was in Alaska, over thirty years ago.

Shortly after mother and dad moved into their new Sun City apartment, I went to visit them. I complimented mother on what an exceptional job she did decorating their new apartment. She had a flair and gift when it came to designing and decorating her home. Their new apartment looked homey. I asked her how she liked living there.

Her response was "Come se, come sa," tilting her head. "Let's go to dinner downstairs in the main dining room and you will see."

I was a guest at the dining hall. There were over fifty tables. Some of the tables were filled with couples but most were not. Most of the tables had groups of ladies, or a man and a few ladies. And there were a few tables where people sat alone. It seemed sad to me.

As we walked towards an empty table, I noticed no one looked at mother or dad as they walked by. No one acknowledged them.

I asked quietly, "Mother, don't you speak to any of these people?"

"They all want to fuck your Father!" she answered loudly enough to get the attention of the other diners. "I know what you all want," she raged with the shark eyes I had seen before, "but he's married to me!" Then she sat down to dine.

I said nothing. Between the institutional style food and the recent incident, dinner was very awkward. Mother recovered herself and inquired how the children were. I didn't feel like making small talk. I thought I would be sick. As we were exiting the dining hall, a woman approached me introducing herself as one of the administrators of the facility. She asked me if I could join her in her office for a moment.

I told my parents I would meet them back in their apartment. The administrator had a look of urgency on her face. People often had a look of urgency when they wanted to speak to me about my mother.

Mother asked what I was doing. I responded by telling her I would be there in a minute. Once the administrator had closed the door to her office, she said that mother had just given their thirty-day notice. They were moving out. This was the first I had heard about another move. Mother hadn't said anything about this at dinner. I asked the administrator where they were moving to. She said she did not know, but she was extremely concerned.

I assumed her concern was for dad. I was wrong. Her concern was for mother. "There is something wrong with your mother, if I can be so bold," she began. "She has a temper that appears in a flash. She continuously yells at the women here." She didn't need to elaborate, I already knew the picture she was painting.

I asked her if she knew what caused mother's yelling. She said mother had a fixation that female residents were interested in "fucking her husband." I could see it was not comfortable for her to share this information with me.

She looked down apologetically. "Of course, we are worried about your father as well. He does not engage in conversation and we are not sure why. She does all the talking for both of them." This I already knew.

Then she added, "We are not sure if your mother does not permit your father to speak or if he has simply retreated inward." I was still processing this last remark when she added, "It appears your mother does not have any boundaries nor does she have any filter. At times, she appears almost psychotic and that behavior is increasing."

I just nodded. I thought she had summed it up perfectly. Once again, I didn't know how to respond, so I thanked her and told her I'd see what I could do. She asked for my cell number to keep in her files. When I returned to their apartment, I didn't need to say much.

Mother said, "So I suppose she told you we are moving." I shook my head in agreement. "I told you all these women want to fuck your father." She continued, "And he doesn't even do anything to try to stop it."

"Mother," I exclaimed, "He doesn't even talk, what do you want him to do?"

"Look", I started, more patiently, "if you get another apartment you are going to have a lot to deal with by yourself. You will need to shop, clean, and you will need to drive." Mother hated driving.

"I don't care! We are moving back to Scottsdale. I already put a deposit down on an apartment. The decision has been made."

With nothing more to say, I hugged them both goodbye and didn't see them again until they moved into their next apartment.

The administrator of the assisted living center in Sun City called me the day before mother and dad moved out. Once again, she shared her concerns and cautioned me they were not a couple who were able to care for themselves. I agreed with her. Thanking her for the call, there was little I could do. Each and every one of these episodes were tortuous. Years before, I realized that kickboxing and step aerobics would help me corral the stress. I worked out five days a week and on the particularly stressful weeks, I planted myself right on the front line of class and pushed myself harder and harder.

Mother called me with their new Scottsdale phone number, along with strict instructions not to give the number out to my cousins or any extended family.

"I never speak to anyone in our family," I reminded her.

When I was sixteen, mother told me that none of my extended family wanted anything to do with me. She said that she had told them off after they criticized my "easy way with the boys and called me a slut". At sixteen, I believed her. But I remained confused since I wasn't a girl that had boyfriends or dated much. Now as an adult, I did not believe much of what mother told me, yet she was still able to hurt my heart. I never pursued relationships with the family I was told wanted nothing to do with me, until later in life.

Shortly, after my parents moved to Scottsdale, I came to Arizona for a conference. When it was over, I drove to mother and dad's new apartment to see how they were doing. They seemed like they were doing as well as could be expected. The apartment was nice and decorated much like the last apartment.

When I inquired about their new life, mother told me their mornings consisted of sitting on their little terrace and having coffee. Then they would come inside for a bowl of cereal and half of a banana.

They would make the decision of what they wanted to have for dinner. Then they would go to the store and get it. Shockingly, dad still drove. I couldn't believe it. Mother would tell him when to go right or left. He followed her commands.

There definitely were moments when I wondered whether dad was more aware of things than he let on, and if he was consciously choosing not to speak. There were times I wondered if he was displaying passive-aggressive type behaviors. I would dismiss that as a ridiculous notion, trying to convince myself he did have dementia.

They would buy only enough groceries to last for one day. After their return from shopping, they would spend the afternoon reading or watching television. After the five o'clock nightly news, they would eat dinner. It was the same regimen every day.

They had no friends, not one. In the earlier years, mother would tell me they would go to a movie once in a while. Eventually, that stopped and they watched movies on television.

I continued to call weekly, but neither of them ever picked up the phone.

Chapter Sixteen:

A Final Image

About a year later, I was asked to present a lecture for the Schools of Criminology and Criminal Justice at the same university I had graduated from, over thirty years before. I was excited to return to Arizona and to return to the university that provided me with such a strong educational and supportive foundation. I flew to Arizona the night before the lecture.

I truly enjoyed having the opportunity to interact with all the enthusiastic students passionate about their upcoming careers. It was joyous to me as I listened to their perceptions and answered questions. Their energy and optimism was contagious. I found myself engaging with them in kind.

The day after the lecture, I drove to see mother and dad unannounced. I knocked on the door. No one answered. I tried the door. It was unlocked. I could hear the television in the living room.

Dad wheeled into the living room from the bedroom. What was he doing in a wheelchair? He was wearing an old pair of pajama bottoms and a very dirty tee shirt. At first, he had a blank stare on his face. Dad squinted to see if it really was me, his daughter, walking through the door. A big smile came over his face. It broke my heart. I had missed my father tremendously.

I approached dad to hug him. That was hard. He reeked of urine and other smells I could not identify. I could hear mother yelling, "Whose there? Who is that?"

I walked into the bedroom. It was in total disarray. Dirty clothes were all over the floor. What I saw next will haunt me until the day I die.

Mother sat up tall in her bed wearing a filthy yellowed cotton nightgown. Her short red hair was spiked out all over her head. When I looked at her, she reminded me of the Joker in the old Batman series.

Her eyes were wild and her face was once again contorted as she raged. "Get out! Get out! You will not put me in a mental hospital!" She continued to pound the bed with her fists yelling, "I will not go! I will not go!"

Mother alternated between uncontrollable screaming and laughing. I did not know this woman, once so beautiful, so confident, so poised, and stylish. Who was this monster in front of me? I was frozen unable to move. How could this happen to a human being, let alone my mother? I felt like I was in a horror movie. I had no idea what to do.

I noticed the living room and bedroom were filled with dumps of feces that looked like some of it had been cleaned up and some had not. I looked at my father and started crying. How could life for this man and woman end like this? They were like dogs living in an unkempt kennel.

All of a sudden, between the smell of the air and my mother shrieking, I felt like I was choking. I couldn't breathe. I needed air. I ran outside trying to ignore her screaming. My mind was in shock. I focused on deep breathing trying to calm down so I could think.

When I returned inside, I headed for the kitchen. As I walked in, I noticed there was duct tape covering the vents in the living room. All the windows were closed and the air conditioning was off. It was over ninety degrees inside and the air was thick and stifling.

I opened up the sliding glass door then looked for a chair I could stand on to remove the duct tapes from the vents. "What are you doing? What are you doing?" yelled mother.

"I am letting some air into this apartment and uncovering the vents so we can get the air conditioning on." "No! No!" she yelled. "The neighbors will be able to hear us if the vents are not covered. They are just waiting to turn us in." I did not respond. Instead I headed to the kitchen and opened the door to the refrigerator. I wasn't sure what I would find; no food or overly spoiled food. I suspected there would not be edible food inside. I was correct. The only food inside their refrigerator was so old and molded; it made the expiration dates unimportant.

The heaviness from all these scenes, dad's sweet smile, mother's physical state in her rage, the vents covered with duct tape, and the molded food in the refrigerator, is still deep within me today. It is a sadness that permeates throughout me. This image takes me to a place that is so macabre, so tragic. They were loved damn it. They had a great family who so desperately wanted to love them but was forced to do so from afar.

I had no idea what to do or where to take my parents. I went back outside their apartment and made several phone calls to my family. I didn't know much about their finances except I remembered them telling me my name was on their accounts. I had no idea which banks had their accounts.

After talking with my family and looking through documents, I became aware that mother and dad were the victims of a fraudulent scam perpetrated on the elderly, especially those with no close family nearby. Mother believed she would outlive dad, so she gave almost all their money, to a 'financial expert' who was in business for himself. He was not with a national company. I was also able to determine there was some monthly income from a few sources, but it wasn't enough to pay their rent, utilities, and food.

I found a cleaning service to do a deep clean in the apartment. Dozens of fresheners were needed to make the air tolerable. I hired an amazing woman who agreed to be their caregiver on a daily basis, seven days a week.

Life changed for mother and dad. Even though dad still wasn't talking, their surroundings improved. Our newfound angel took mother and dad to their appointments, made sure their clothes were clean, and there was food in the refrigerator. In addition, she cooked for them.

Much to our surprise and delight, mother liked her. She liked her a lot until the day she didn't. When mother turned on her caregiver, she raged about reporting her to the Attorney General's Office and the police department. The sweet woman broke down in tears and called me. Mother was also accusing her caregiver of stealing from them.

Their caregiver had lasted a few months before mother drove her out. I believed I was fortunate to have found such an amazing professional to put up with mother's ranting and dad's retreat inward. I was truly sad to lose her. Once again, I apologized for mother's behavior, assured the caregiver, there would not be any complaints filed against her. I'd write an Affidavit in support of her if need be.

I paid her a final check and never heard from her again. I will always be grateful to this sweet angel for the love and care she gave to mother and dad. After their caregiver went away in tears, the only option was of a more impersonal nature. I hired a series of caregivers from an elder care agency to come by three to four times a week. This way mother did not get too close to any one of them.

They stocked the refrigerator with ready- made meals and snack type foods to sustain mother and dad. Sometimes, they cooked an extra dinner for one night to last for several meals.

It proved to be a temporary fix. Just a few months later, I was chest deep in work building my consulting business along with finishing a nine-month contract. I hadn't had a day off in months.

One Saturday afternoon, I was able to come up for air. One of my daughters was seven months pregnant and we were in the middle of throwing her a baby shower. I was eagerly anticipating the birth of my fourth grandchild.

It was a beautiful sunny day. The view of the mountains was truly breathtaking. We could see eagles perched in the trees all around us. This was a perfect afternoon for a celebration.

As my daughter started opening gifts, my cell phone rang. Normally, I would not have answered my phone during such a special occasion. I have absolutely no idea why I picked up. The caller ID showed unknown. "Mother trouble breathing."

"Dad? Dad?" I yelled. I hadn't heard his voice in decades. "Call 911 and I will too."

I hung up the phone and immediately called 911. I don't know if dad did the same. I didn't think he could talk. Mother was taken by ambulance to a hospital nearby. She was diagnosed with pulmonary embolisms. They stabilized her in the Emergency Room then admitted her.

I was on the phone with the emergency room staff almost continually for the next few hours. Dad had ridden with mother in the ambulance. The Staff in the emergency room explained dad seemed disoriented. He did not speak or answer any of their questions.

They didn't know what to do with dad. I asked them to put him on the phone. "Dad, you need to listen to me. Mother needs to stay in the hospital for a few nights. The hospital attendant is going to put you in a taxi." I repeated that again.

"Do you understand me, dad?" I asked praying he would. "Yes," he responded. I was so thankful he was engaged with me, I didn't have time to analyze it. "I am giving the attendant your address. Go in the house and go to sleep. I will get someone there in the morning. Please pick up your phone when it rings."

I repeated these directions several times, asking him if he understood what I had just said. Several times, he responded, "Yes."

I guess my fourth repetition really got him when he answered, "OK Susie babe." I was dumbfounded. Quickly rebounding, I prayed he would follow my directions.

I called a family friend to stay with dad. Then I arranged for the elder care providers to come in on a daily basis starting the next morning. I called dad the next morning and our friend answered the phone.

He cared for dad that entire day and drove him back to the hospital so he could see my mother. I was making plans to get to Arizona as fast as we could. It was summertime in Alaska, therefore flights with short notice were either totally booked or enormously expensive.

Once mother stabilized, even more problems began. She started cursing and when dad came to visit, she started yelling, "Get the fuck out of my room! "I hate you!" They sent dad home.

Mother started punching the nurses as they got close to her. She spat on them and yelled vulgar obscenities at them, disturbing all the patients around her. I was told her yelling was uncontrollable. An immediate psychiatric evaluation was ordered.

After the first psychiatrist evaluated mother, he immediately requested a second psychiatric evaluation. I later learned that was to support the first one. They wanted two different professionals evaluating her since they were aghast at what they learned.

No one could get near mother. They had to medicate her to put her into a straight- jacket. When she awoke, they set her a chair in the nurse's station until they could decide what to do with her. The supervisor of the hospital's social workers called me. She was firm and direct with me. My mother was now in a hoodie covering her head since she continued spitting on any staff near the nurse's station. The visual of this broke my heart into a million pieces. I wanted to break down at that moment. It took all of my inner strength and dig deep to hear my inner voice so I could move forward. I negotiated with myself that I could feel anything

I wanted later, but now I had to be efficient and effective. The compassion and confusion had to be placed on the shelf for a little while as I tried to conceptualize the enormity of what the doctors shared with me.

"Both psychiatrists have diagnosed your mother with a Stage 4 Borderline Personality Disorder. We are giving you forty-five minutes to get here (to Arizona) and accept guardianship of her or we are moving her to the State's Geriatric Psychiatric Hospital."

"What does that mean to take guardianship?" I asked. The anxious social worker advised me there were professionals available in the Phoenix area to help us navigate through the enormous legal and medical systems we were about to enter.

I was so shocked by this news, my response was, "and my daughter is going to have a baby soon." I begged the social worker to give me a little more time since I was still in Alaska. This was too big of a decision to make in forty-five minutes. She was emphatic, "No, I do not have any leeway here. You have forty-five minutes." I honestly could not blame her or any of the hospital staff.

I tried to explain that this was such a big decision and I couldn't make it in forty-five minutes. Again, she strongly advised me to call one of the three elder care professionals she had referred me to who could help me navigate this complicated web.

Before she hung up, she repeated again, "You have forty-five minutes."

"Wait, wait, wait," I yelled, "What about my father? Is he there right now?" "No," she answered, "we aren't allowing him up here. They sent him home earlier. She is too violent. She's having psychotic episodes."

This truly felt like a horror movie. I was given only forty-five minutes to decide whether my mother was being taken to a state run psychiatric hospital or find an alternative. I was paralyzed and reminded myself to breathe so I could think. But nothing came except a wave of great sadness.

My pregnant daughter walked into the room at exactly the right time. I fell into her arms, sobbing as I told her the fate that was awaiting my mother, her grandmother. No matter how difficult my life had been with her, I never would have wished this on her. I felt tortured by the position both mother and I were in.

My daughters became my support as I navigated this nightmare. Once I composed myself, I telephoned my family and friends. My next call was to one of the companies on the referral list. It was a good call under the circumstances. The owner made himself available to me for over an hour answering one question after another. I was on the phone with him and I missed the forty-five- minute deadline. Totally consumed, I realized I'd missed most of the baby shower.

Initially, I tried to explain to the man on the other end of the phone that this was not an ordinary referral. I tried to explain our extenuating circumstances. By the end of this case, several months later, he told me this was the hardest case he'd ever had.

He told me it would take $20,000 to take guardianship of both mother and dad. I found the entire process to be convoluted and overwhelming. Since mother was incapacitated and declared mentally unfit, it fell to dad. Since dad was able to speak only a few words at a time, I was forced to take a look at a guardianship for him as well. That translated to $5,000 to pay the attorney for the person taking guardianship of mother and another $5,000 to gain guardianship of dad. I had to find that money immediately.

Apparently, when someone requests legal guardianship over an individual, they must also hire and pay for a separate attorney to represent the interests of the allegedly incapacitated person. In our case, it translated to another $5,000 to hire an attorney for mother, and $5,000 to hire an attorney for dad. All parties required their own representation. I had to find $20,000 immediately.

I flew to Arizona and made extended arrangements for dad to have round the clock care. He alternated between states of agitation or being completely withdrawn. His caregivers worked hard while we navigated the world of geriatric psychiatric issues for both of them. The hospital social worker was true to her word. Since I had not made arrangements for mother within the allotted forty-five minutes, she was moved to the geriatric psychiatric hospital run by the state. I knew dad was settled with a caregiver.

I was finally able to get a flight from Alaska to Arizona. Directly after getting off the plane, I rented a car and went to see mother. She was heavily medicated. As I walked in the door, even in her drug induced stupor, she said, "Oh you may look good, but you are still a bitch. You finally did something with that hair."

And for the first time in my life, I was able to look at her with kindness and a smile, "Thanks mother. It's all going to be ok."

It was at that moment that I finally understood that the mother I had dealt with for over fifty years was a seriously ill woman rather than a mother who appeared to me as a monster. I was able to look beyond the trauma and chaos she had caused and see a deeply broken human being.

Even with all the drugs they injected into her, she still looked at me with those same shark eyes, so characteristic of borderline psychosis.

Out in the hallway, with her door shut, the psychiatrist discussed what was happening with mother. They planned to keep her for a while and evaluate her situation.

He then gave me an added bonus. They wanted to admit dad, too, since they had no idea what was wrong with him. Apparently, the caregivers had brought dad to visit mother before my plane landed.

He would not speak or respond to hospital staff during his brief visit. They were concerned about his mental health as well. I continued to feel extremely overwhelmed and remained speechless. I wanted to ask the doctor if he had some medication for me as well, but I didn't think that was the appropriate response. Instead, I thanked the doctor and said I'd take his suggestion under advisement.

After the hospital, I ran over to meet and pay all the various attorneys so we could start the guardianship process. I returned to the apartment to check on dad.

I arrived at the apartment just as there was a change of caregivers by the agency caring for dad. I assured dad everything was going to be all right. I just needed him to give me a little time. I spoke with the next caregiver and made sure there was food for her to prepare for dad's dinner. I hugged dad and left.

By the end of that day, after checking into my hotel room, I collapsed on the bed feeling totally depleted. I didn't want to think about what the next day would bring.

Chapter Seventeen:

Finally At Peace

If I had to use one word to describe the next week it would be nightmare.

While the doctors were evaluating and treating mother's mental health issues, mother collapsed and started bleeding. She was rushed by ambulance to another hospital in downtown Phoenix. Those doctors found she was also bleeding internally.

It was the middle of the night when the staff at the State's Geriatric Psychiatric Hospital alerted me to mother's condition. The nurse explained they were not equipped to handle both psychiatric and physical issues at their facility, so they had moved her yet again.

Soon after her admittance to the new hospital in downtown Phoenix, mother was diagnosed with colon cancer. It had spread throughout her body. The doctors were skeptical whether she was a surgical candidate given the quality and quantity of her life post surgery. The team suggested we consider palliative care as an option.

I supported that decision. While the logistical planning was challenging, the care options were actually made easier for us. Finding an assisted living facility that accepted a resident with physical illnesses was easier to place than those with psychiatric issues. Her physical issues were now considered primary.

The only problem was that the hospital would only keep mother in the Palliative Care Unit for forty-eight hours. I felt like I was on a constant race against the clock with these finish lines being totally unattainable.

I had learned to take these professionals at their word. With mother, they were not messing around. Forty-eight hours meant just that.

I shuddered to think of what they would do with her if an assisted living home was not found within that timeframe, I expected they would move her to the county hospital.

Dad's caregiver had brought him to the hospital to visit mother just as I was told of her prognosis. Dad and I went to get a cup of coffee.

After taking a few gulps of this much-needed coffee, I explained to dad that mother was not well and needed to live in an assisted living facility. I had no idea if he would converse with me or even understand what I was saying. He had not spoken to me in decades.

Dad responded with a few words, "Stay with her." I looked at him in total shock.

"Stay with her. Together," he repeated. "I will move."

"Are you sure?" I asked more out of my own shock that he was actually talking and engaging with me. He seemed cognitively aware and able to process what I was talking about.

"Yes," was all he said and he drank his coffee. I squeezed his hand and told him everything would be ok. His request became the mission.

I found an assisted living facility where both mother and dad could live. Between hospice care and elder care professionals, mother and dad had people surrounding them round the clock.

Doctors had given mother five to six more months. Until then I had a lot to do. Now that the expedited guardianship papers had been filed, the next step was to move their belongings out of their apartment and get them settled in the assisted living home.

The combination of tending to both mother and dad was quite a lot for the assisted living center to handle. So, I hired an independent caregiver named Thomas to assist. He would sing to mother and dad and joke with them. What a treasure we found with him. Now funds were needed for four attorneys, an assisted living center, and 24-hour care.

Once they were moved in and became familiar with the facility, I returned home to Alaska, needing to once again find some balance and normalcy after the insanity of the last weeks. I hoped to return home and have at least one day to relax. My brain felt so overloaded and overwhelmed, I was totally depleted. I needed to restore myself physically and mentally. Yet, I could not shake this unsettling feeling inside me. It was not the exhaustion or grief. It was something deeper than that.

I felt this intense need for mother to know she was loved. Even though our lives were a series of continuous, never ending roller coaster rides, and even though she was psychotic and frightening, she was still my mother. The tumultuous years of my life with her needed to be set aside for a little while, while I gave my mother one last gift.

I called each of my children. I wanted mother to have a chance to see me, her grandchildren, and great-grandchildren together. They were her family, but she barely knew them. I had buffered them from her for most of their childhoods.

On this last leg of her journey, I was adamant that she didn't feel like she was alone. I told each of my children to pack a bag with a week's worth of clothing for themselves, their spouses, and each of their children. We were all flying down to Phoenix the next day. Surprisingly, we were all on the same flights except my son who flew in from back east.

The next night, I checked back into the hotel that I'd stayed at frequently in the prior months. This time, we secured four rooms instead of one. Hotel staff was amazing with us and by this time we were all on a first name basis. After dropping off all our bags in our hotel rooms, we crammed into two rental cars and drove over to the assisted living center where both mother and dad now resided. I had made a total of seventeen trips from Alaska to Arizona in three years. Had I realized I was going to continually return, I would have surely purchased a condo and bought a car. It would have been infinitely cheaper!

We walked into mother and dad's apartment all together. They did a double take. I hugged both of my parents and told them I brought everyone to Phoenix for a family reunion. I knew that mother and I could never undo the decades of the past. Yet, it was important to me for my mother see how much she was loved one last time. She cried as each person in the family came up to give her a hug. She had tears in her eyes. I didn't see any evidence of shark eyes, only joy.

My oldest daughter hugged mother and introduced her to her husband and her two young daughters, mother's great-granddaughters. My daughter had been eight months pregnant at the time, barely allowed to still fly. She placed mother's hand on her stomach. "Grandma, and this is your great-grandson."

Then my middle daughter came to give her grandmother a hug. She introduced mother to her husband. Mother had spoken to him on the phone a few times, but had never met him. When he hugged mother, she said, "I've always liked this guy," as she smiled. Their little boy, mother's first great grandson, gave her and dad a big hug, and climbed on dad's lap, just talking away and playing with his beard.

Then my son hugged the grandmother he hadn't known much in his life.

I gave my mother another hug and said, "Mother, this is your family. You are loved." This is a memory I will never forget.

With tears in her eyes, she said, "You always said you were going to have a big family."

"Yes, WE are a big family," I said joyously encircling my arms around all in the room.

"I wish we could have had this reunion earlier," She said sadly.

"Me too mom, me too," I said, turning away so she wouldn't see my tears.

I had become proficient at being tough and hiding tears. I had always been cautious not to show my vulnerabilities, fearful she'd come in for the kill. Yet, she still broke my heart. Mother wanted so badly to love and be loved.

Between her extreme lack of boundaries and lack of filter, her roller coaster rides, and her psychotic episodes, it was unsafe for her to be around children. Despite driving us away, she deeply longed for our love. I found that to be a 'deep rooted' sadness that I still grapple with to this day.

We had a lovely time that afternoon, eating ice cream and laughing. Ice cream was all mother was able to keep down, so we got her favorite, a cup of mint chip. The young children had no understanding of mother's ways. Their young innocence brought a level of calm to what had previously been sheer hell.

The next night, while mother was sleeping, we took dad out to dinner at The Cheesecake Factory. Mother was sleeping more and more now.

We were a huge crowd. Dad started talking more and more. "Tell me everything about your lives, everything I have missed," he said clearly, smiling from ear to ear. His oldest granddaughter broke down in tears still holding dear, the fond, but distant memories she had of her "Poppy." She hugged him and he soothed her like he did when she was little.

Once we all dried our tears, each child, spouse, and grandchild said a little something about their lives to share with their Poppy. We made a toast to Poppy and once again there was not a dry eye at the table.

When it was time to order, I asked dad what he would like for dinner. He smiled and said, "I have no idea. I have not ordered in a restaurant in a very long time. You order me something, Susie-babe, and I will love it." I ordered him his favorite, a hamburger well done and he loved it.

After spending a week with mother and dad, it was time for us all to leave. We left the same way we arrived. All of us drove to the assisted living home to say goodbye.

Each person in our family gave them hugs. When half of our group had said their goodbyes, and the other half was standing nearby, I looked over at mother and did a double take. She was starting to escalate.

Turning her head to look at me, I recognized those piercing shark eyes I knew only too well. One of my daughters was standing next to me, seeing the same image of mother.

The calmness was short lived and mother started screaming, "You never thought we loved you. That one," she said pointing her finger at me. "That one doesn't think she was ever loved," she started her ranting aimed at the disappointment I was in her life. Her yelling became louder and louder. The veins became visible on the face that had now become so gaunt.

My daughter quietly said, "Now I understand why you protected us from her."

"Ok mother," I stepped in. "We have to go now." I reached over to attempt to give her a hug, but I could see she could not handle that. She pulled from me with absolute distain. I did not know this would be the last time I would see my mother. I thought she had more time.

"Take care mother, I will see you soon," was the last thing I said to my mother. I planned to return a few weeks later for a long weekend. I gently ushered everyone out the door. Mother was not in a good state. Experience told me she was escalating and would soon blow up, before eventually calming herself down. There was little I could do to prevent this cascade of events.

Being the last one to leave the room, I told them, and their caregiver Thomas that I would return in a few weeks since there was a long, four-day weekend coming up. I would fly to Phoenix to see mother and dad then.

Even on her deathbed, I was still hoping her episodes would subside. Perhaps I was wishing for something she wasn't capable of controlling.

I always wondered if she could control the escalated spewing.

I hugged dad. He walked down to the lobby with us.

"Thank you," he said. "I love you Susie Babe."

We returned home to Alaska and forty-eight hours later, at 2:30am, mother died. As she was taking her last breath, dad laid alongside her, holding her hand.

I turned right around and flew back to Arizona. I did not find her death difficult. I believed she found in death what she would not find in life, peace.

For me, her funeral was the hardest to cope with. I experienced a raw sadness that sat deep within me. It felt like my heart was bleeding. Planning her funeral was one of the most difficult moments in my life.

Initially, I did not want to be the one to make all the arrangements for her funeral. I felt exhausted, confused, and totally overwhelmed. I needed to grieve not just for her death, but the way our family lived for decades.

I still had no idea what had transpired with dad. Upon mother's death, he started talking and engaging in conversation. I found all of it unbearable and heartbreaking, mourning the time lost, and empty relationships.

I had always thought that my mother's death would be one of the more freeing moments of my life. I was wrong. I would be tested one more time in the future. That would provide me a sense of freedom.

For the first time in my entire life, I felt like I wasn't strong enough to face the responsibilities that laid ahead of me. Besides feeling like I would collapse from total exhaustion, I really just wanted to run away.

I had been good at doing that. If I didn't want to deal with chronic problems from my mother, I just left.

This time, I couldn't walk away. My mother died. I needed to find the words to show respect to my mother in her eulogy. I struggled and after several hours, the only words I wrote on my paper were, "She is at peace." Mother had alienated absolutely everyone in her life. There was no one to invite to the funeral. It troubled me at my core, that she could live a life for seventy-five years and no one wanted to mourn her passing. How ironic, I was the one to eulogize mother at her funeral. It came full circle.

I worked for two days on the eulogy. It was not going well. On the third night, I went out for a walk and it came to me. Giving my mother this eulogy was going to be my final gift to mother, from the daughter who hated and loved her all of my life.

I embraced the intimacy of this small memorial and gave us both a gift; seeing the wonder and brilliance of this wounded woman through my father's eyes. Dad stood by mother until her very last breath.

Many of my memories of my mother were not good ones. Even though mother was mean and nasty, and no one wanted to be around her in life or death, I knew her life had purpose. I saw the faces of both of my grandmothers and remembered what they had taught me. I had to be authentic and I needed to be strong.

As I stood next to my mother's coffin, I surprised myself. I felt a sense of honor. I had the clarity I had not had for so much of my life. This would be the final tribute to my mother. I would honor the life of this pained human being. I was the daughter who desperately wanted to show her mother she loved her, but could not. I spoke to my mother in death, the way I wish I could have spoken to her in life.

I gathered four white roses, one for each of her great-grandchildren. As I laid each one on top of her coffin, I thanked her for their existence and of generations to come, all because of her. Then I told her a little about each one of her great grandchildren.

I gathered peach roses, one for each of her grandchildren and their spouses. As I laid each one on top of her coffin, I gave her thanks, and told her a little about each of them, and the amazing people they are.

I gathered orange roses and spoke of her family. I thanked mother for my life and let her know that no matter the past, she was my mother and I loved her.

And lastly, I gathered a bouquet of red roses on behalf of dad. He laid them on her coffin as I read a poem about loyalty and devotion.

My mother taught me to read, not words, she taught me to read eyes. She taught me to read shark eyes, mean eyes, sad eyes, blank eyes, and kind eyes. She gave me the gift of a hyper-vigilant sensitivity which in turn allowed me to develop a grounded sense of calm. This has led me well in my career as a criminologist. It wasn't purely all the degrees I held that taught me success professionally, it was my mother. Books cannot teach people what I know and how I respond to scenes. I work in a world of rage and violence. I am not uncomfortable in that world.

As with other children of borderline parents, we can read each other. These children, young or old, can look into my eyes and we connect. Many feel safety and validation they have lacked in their own lives.

This is the gift my mother gave to me. To dedicate my life to working with children, some of who are just like me.

Chapter Eighteen:

Family Ever After

Father loved his wife.
    He loved my mother.

He loved her smile, her sparkling eyes, and her sense of style and flair.

He loved how beautifully she sang and the goofy faces she could make when she was joking around.

He loved how she would flirt with him after they had an argument, and then she'd sing to him, "What's It All About, Alfie?" That was her pet name for him after an argument.

Dad loved and saw mother in a way no one else did. He understood the root of her pain.

He held on to her during the rough episodes and cherished those moments when they could play together as friends and lovers.

Dad loved me, his daughter. He loved the family he created.

Most of his life, dad grew up with a single mother, who was seldom home because of her work. To him, family had been an enigma just beyond his reach. Once he created a family of his own, he would not let it go. What he couldn't foresee was the incredible toll mother's episodes took on the rest of the family.

Once I left home at the young age of seventeen, I began to catch my breath. I felt peace. I developed a voice. What stayed with me was the distorted way I saw day to day events and the world. I continue to be driven towards social causes and injustices. It filled my soul. But I was stunted in my development to understand relationships. I didn't give up, met some wonderful men, and tried to make sense of what was in front of me. I met a lot of wolves who confused me. I wasted too much time trying to make sense of that, yet thankfully spent equal time developing my professional self. And that was wildly successful and enriching. As I became an adult about to turn forty, I realized that I spent so much time navigating what was in front of me, in constant fight or flight mode that I didn't develop the depth I was seeking. So, I went on that journey to find myself deep within. It was at that time, I was able to see and understand my mother through my father's eyes. He paid a huge price for that love. He endured trauma that was relentless. I would not have made the same choice, but I was able to recognize that he had moments and memories of great love.

I believe Dad recognized the tumultuousness of our house, the frequent roller coaster rides, and the constant states of confusion, especially as I started to get older and moved out of the house. I am not sure he recognized mother's lack of boundaries. He seemed to ignore her lack of filter and walk away. That was not the case for me.

I've come to realize that for dad, early on, there was enough joy and laughter with his wife, to augment the constant explosive screaming that would come up without provocation or warning.

Even after she died, dad told me, with tears in his eyes, that he understood more than I'd realized over the years. She was the love of his life until the day she died.

He would smile remembering all the good things about mother. He absorbed the pain of her psychotic episodes. Yet he was always waiting for her on the other side, always trying to catch her as she fell.

Dad understood mother in a way no one else could and at a level no one could. He knew she was a wounded bird, not a heartless monster.

He would never leave her. There came a day when it became too much for him and he needed to love her from afar, not by leaving her, but by retreating inward.

It cost dad greatly to stay with the woman he loved. He lost years with his daughter, his grandchildren, his sister and brother, his nieces and nephews.

His heart was joyous for the family they created together, fragmented as it was. We were his very own real family.

Dad held tenaciously to that idea at all costs, even at the cost of losing his own voice. Dad made a promise to love my mother forever and he did. He held her hand as she took her final breath.

Dad dated several women during this three years at the assisted living center assuring me "he never went further than walking them to their door". I chuckled, encouraging him to walk through those doors! And one day, after spending a good amount of time exclusively with one woman, he called me asking me I had heard anything about her. "She's not here anymore, Susie-babe. I wonder if she died."

My heart broke. "I'll be there soon dad". That was all I could think to say. I later learned, she had died.

My father lived for three more years in the same apartment he shared with my mother when she died. During those three years, I was fortunate to see him for a week at a time, every three months.

Each time I heard his voice, I had an emotional pull at my heart. I wonder if he knew I had to force back the tears every time I hugged him hello. I had missed my dad.

We had some of our best conversations during those three years. They resonate with me still today. Dad gave me two gifts. After mother passed away, he regained his voice. To hear his kind voice once again and hear his laughter was the most precious gift of all, or so I thought.

Dad gave me another gift in those three years. He gave me the ability to love and forgive my mother through his eyes. Dad and I would sit in the library at the assisted living home and remember joyous moments with mother.

We laughed as we remembered her dancing to the new 45 records I had just bought, swinging me around and showing me her fancy dance steps. We remembered how she sang as she walked down each of the isles at the grocery store, ignoring our embarrassment. We smiled remembering the Wednesday night "Dancing On Skates" classes they took together for years.

Once a year, mother and dad would take me into the city to see a Broadway Show. We would dine on a six-course meal at Mama Leone's before each show. I loved that time with both of them. It was one of the very few memories I have of us together laughing and feeling free.

We reminisced how much mother loved to shop. She had a sense of style and flair few could achieve. She was glamorous and beautiful. And when she was in a calm state, her eyes glistened with happiness. She was beautiful. My mother was beautiful. I could see that now.

Mother's infectious laughter was a trait I inherited. How lucky for me to have inherited her way to lighten the soul so completely. I miss my mother's laughter and wish we could have shared more of those moments together. Now, as time has passed, everything is no longer locked in a compartment in my mind, numbing and dismissing the painful parts of my life. Now, I am capable of remembering some of the joys.

Mother was amazing in so many ways. Dad saw that and loved her for it. Mother had what many want, a loving partner who adored her and stayed by her side for over fifty-five years.

Dad lightened my heart, inviting me to see my tumultuous life with mother another way, through his loving eyes.

The three years I had with dad were more than I ever thought I would have. I was grateful, but it wasn't enough. I thought we would have more time.

His last words to me were, "You are OK, Susie Babe. I love you. I am good. I have to let you go now."

He died five hours later, fifteen days before I was to see him again.

Epilogue

*W*hy would I tell this story? Writing about 'my life' was difficult at the most visceral level. Early on, I thought I grew up "normal" just like everyone else. While I sensed some things were amiss as I entered adolescence, I did not know exactly what was wrong. I just knew my life felt like a roller coaster ride that never seemed to stop. Day to day I felt more horrible than I felt good. I felt sad more than I felt happy. I hid that by trying to always have a smile on my face. It was a facade. I tried harder and harder to make my life and my mother happier, but I never could, until the day she died. As she neared the end of her life, I was able to understand her and her behaviors. It took time to forgive the traumatic memories and absurdity that was part of my life. Understanding my mother had a chronically traumatic and complex childhood without interventions or relief, made my own journey of forgiveness more palpable.

Even though I felt sick to my stomach much of the time I was writing this story, I was compelled to share this story with others; professionals, adults, and other grown children, so maybe their journey could be more understood. I have limited memories of experiences most children remember, like birthdays, Thanksgivings, and other holidays and traditions. For me, only a small bag of photos is my reference to parts of my life. There are no photos of my birthdays, of my graduation, or of my wedding reception. My own bank of photos has only become plentiful once I married and started my own family.

The more that professionals attended my lectures and gained insight into this world, the more people reached out to me thanking me for helping them to make sense of their own lives. They often shared stories not dissimilar to mine. Every lecture I gave about this specific type of trauma brought me more and more of an understanding that while still rare, the situation of growing up with a borderline personality disorder parent impacted a good number of youth. Yet, this type of trauma, or many others, is not taught to professionals, even to this day. This drove me and propelled me to aid others in understanding, so they could step in and help these children, so many who have been like me.

In my earlier years, there were only two professionals who understood there was something very wrong in my house. One was my high school counselor who facilitated in getting me scholarships and academic opportunities so I could change the trajectory of my life. The other was my university advisor, a retired FBI agent. I often credit him for the work I am able to do with young people today, who are dealing with trauma. He saw the trauma in my eyes, gently prodded more and more out of me. Ultimately, he was able to set me on an unusual career path I was destined for, even though I was not able to see the path at that time. I will always be eternally grateful to these two men.

In my later years, I had to grieve me, mourn this little girl, this teen, this young woman. And ultimately in turn, I was able to grieve for my mother and the inner conflict and turmoil she endured for a lifetime. If I can prevent one young person from enduring this trauma, I will continue to tell this story, excruciating as it is for me. If one professional can identify a child or adolescent that lives a life with a borderline, this is worth it. I have taught professionals about a concept I call incongruence. There may be a smile on the face but look at the eyes. Do they match the expression on the face? Once I had a very close friend say to me, "You are sad." "No, I'm happy. I'm good," I insisted. She took my hand and said, "but not with your eyes."

Additionally, I have been able to teach professionals about daydreaming. Sometimes when a child is daydreaming they are giving their brains the rest they so desperately need because they feel safe with you. They do not feel this safety in their homes. I understand this well and find myself daydreaming, still today, giving their brain a rest so.

Oftentimes, I have been asked about my education in regards to my work. I am well educated with graduate degrees and certificated credentials, but that is the wrong question. The question should be how do I know so much about this subject? I come out strong on the other side And the answer is that I really must credit my mother, not just with my successful career, but for my ability to see what so many miss or are unaware of. My mother taught me how to read eyes and how to read the energy and air surrounding people. I learned to become confident in my sixth sense and to trust my gut. I became a master at those techniques that simply cannot be taught at school. I don't look for violence or aggression, but I learned to become a master at navigating a world of rage and trauma, and feel comfortable in it. I am able to center myself and be grounded as all around me is falling apart. That cannot be taught in school. Over time, I learned to become confident that I can overcome, coming out strong on the other end. Many who work and study with me tell me that they are calmed by my quiet strength during some of the most horrific moments of their lives. I understand their words.

Additionally, this enabled me to be able to work inside maximum security prisons; aware of my surroundings, but strong in my presence. This allowed me to be able to really see inmates in a way few ever have. No excuse for their crimes, but they are able to articulate their trauma with me. Conversely, this also allowed me to work with borderlines who were so aggressive they ultimately lost their freedom because of their rage. Their stories, the lives that they shared with me allowed me, as a criminologist, to gain an understanding of the development of their journeys. Many broke down in tears not understanding what happened to them or why they felt so out of control in their lives. While this does not dismiss their actions or intentions, it does provide answers and sometimes peace not only just to them, but also to some of their victims. Victims often have the same simple question, why? Why did this crime happen? For many, understanding the internal pain that changed the lives of so many in their path has brought some relief. I have felt honored to play a small part in this process. And while I would not wish this on anyone, I owe my understanding and ability to work with such an injured population to my mother, because it was she who provided me the best education of all.

Not long ago, I had a person who was very close to me tell me that I presented as a blend of a forever child; while still functioning, and thriving as an adult. He'd never known anyone who exhibited both of these roles simultaneously. I have come to explain this to those who study with me as stunted development. Parts of the emotional me will forever be a child, while the rest of my being was able to mature and thrive. I've grown to become comfortable with this child inside me, showing her grace and gentleness as I understand her and me. I can vacillate from silly and funny to focused and on point. I have been told a few times, You don't seem like an investigator. I always ask, what is an investigator supposed to be like? If I was always a serious and stern person all the time, I would have missed out on so many amazing things people have shared with me. I continue to be attuned to the child within me while allowing my door to be open for others to feel comfortable to "talk to me". That has been a real benefit of my stunted development; I have one foot on both sides.

For my dear mother, the tragedy was that she had everything; beauty, a husband who adored and worshiped her, and a family who desperately wanted to love her, yet she pushed them all away. My mother was a beautiful woman; always fashionably stylish and impeccable. In time, I was able to see and appreciate her beauty in a way that I could not before. She lived a life that was financially secure. She attained so many of the pieces in life that we all strive to achieve, yet all of which she was never able to appreciate and accept, due to her disorder. Not understanding, this left many around her confused. She alienated an extended family who would have loved to be a part of her life had she allowed it. My mother wasn't able to fully appreciate what she yearned for, or acknowledge the love that others tried to have for her. Her life was so rich, yet she was never able to grasp this.

The diversity of our wonderful family, the talents she passed down to all of us, and her many grandchildren and great-grandchildren. They are now able to grow up more whole, complete, and healthy because we were able to break the cycle of trauma. Instead of being bitter and angry, we can now understand her inner turmoil. We wish we could have been part of her healing instead of needing protection from her.

I broke the cycle of trauma by preventing the continuation of trauma from the relationship which was so psychotic. While the cycle was broken, the sadness remains from the loss of what could have been.

If my story resonates with you, I hope you find the peace and healing I have been able to find over time. If you recognize a young person from my story, reach out to them. You truly can change the trajectory of their life. My life is glorious because of those who reached out to me. I have spectacular children whom I not only love, but like. I love their spouses. I have grandchildren who make my heart burst watching their enthusiasm, curiosity, and most of all their smiles. I have had great loves in my life; their gifts did not go unappreciated. My life has been filled with such purpose that even as I age and my body gets older and tired, I know I still have more to give as we navigate the unprecedented residuals from these modern times.

I have led a blessed and fortunate life in many respects, because of those who reached out to me. I have been able to Break the Cycle of Trauma Through A Daughter's Eyes.

Stages of Borderline Personality Disorder

There are four stages or types of Borderline Personality Disorder. Stage One is the mildest version of this disorder directed more inward. Stage Four is the most severe and the most violent and directed more outward. The very impetus is based on the fear of being left alone, yet those afflicted drive those around them away. I am the child of a Stage Four Borderline Mother.

Many professionals do not want to treat borderlines. It took over fifty years for my mother to finally get the attention of professionals and people in the community. Before that, she kept her behaviors carefully hidden behind closed doors. Some might say she controlled them until she couldn't.

Most professionals do not know about the trauma children or spouses of borderlines experience, yet the trauma can be incomprehensible. We are a nation focusing on trauma, therefore it is imperative this disorder be taught and acknowledged so there can be change. Children of borderlines can break the generational trauma they are chronically exposed to if only the professionals working with them knew about it. Many people presenting with borderline personality disorder have deeply rooted trauma themselves. Their psychotic raging is selective. Their prey experience chronic and complex trauma, which can be broken, so in turn it does not get passed on to their children so the cycle doesn't continue. The jury is still out as to whether to consider borderline personality disorder a product of nature verses nurture. Most professionals in the field of psychology and criminology will agree that Borderline Personality Disorder is one of the most difficult personality disorders to change.

I became my mother's first target, followed by my father. Others in the family were not her prey. Some might prefer to refer to us as her victims, but I don't see myself as a victim. With the support of family, teachers, counselors, and other professionals, I was able to Break the Cycle of Trauma. My father was not as fortunate.

We didn't talk about mental health or personality disorders when I was a child. I never even knew what it was, until I became a criminologist. I wish I knew then, what I know now. Perhaps we would not have been so confused, guilty, and traumatized.

A person who has a borderline personality disorder will change their behavior in a matter of seconds. As they age, I have observed they may get worse. Others inside and outside the house may not notice or understand the signs or behaviors the borderline is displaying to others even if they observe it. The borderline is brilliant at timing. Everything can look wonderful to those looking in from the outside. It is quite the opposite once you come through the door.

Most professionals are not trained to identify or work with borderlines or their families. Only those professionals specifically trained in this disorder can identify the struggles of their children and spouses. The child or spouse may be clothed, fed, and appear like all is well, but if you look at their eyes they will have sad eyes or blank eyes and expressions. Even when they smile, there will be a dichotomy between what the face is showing and the eyes are saying. Believe the eyes.

How do these targeted children present? Since they are experiencing a series of never-ending roller coaster rides, the ups and downs of emotions becomes too much so they learn not to feel. They learn to just be in that moment and not to show emotion. They fear if they show their vulnerabilities, the borderline parent will use that against them in their next psychotic episode. The borderline will use those very vulnerabilities, to rip apart their children or their spouses, as they rage uncontrollably. Overtime, as that child increases the need to numb, the numbing permeates more and more of their lives. Numbing becomes less selectively controlled and the child of the borderline will start not to feel more and more aspects of their lives. In that process, they lose the sense of self they still have remaining. They often don't grow and develop emotionally as most children do. They live in a perpetual state of fight or flight, which can cause stunted development for some. I have been told by several different people close to me that I have an interesting blend of adult and a child that has not grown up.

The borderline parent does not protect, nurture, or keep her children safe. This is the child's normal; they believe all families are like this so they adjust. In order to survive, these children either crack or get tough so they can survive until they reach adulthood. Both ways have their repercussions.

Life for these children can be tortuous. This life style has often been compared to those who were prisoners in a concentration camp. Yet still, most professionals never learn about this disorder in their training.

Living in this type of acute, chronic trauma affects the youth throughout their childhood, adolescence and into their adult years. This child will try to please their parent in every way possible. Yet, there will be no way this child can meet this parent's demands. The child does not understand this, so they try harder and harder.

The borderline parent may have several children. The treatment is oftentimes not equal amongst the siblings. This adds another layer of confusion and insecurity to the targeted child. There is research being done questioning why some siblings become the target and others do not.

Most of the targeted children and adults don't speak about what has occurred in their homes. For starters, they don't know what to say. This is the only normal they know. Additionally, the borderline parent can be extremely intimidating to any professionals working with their children or family, fearing the professional is getting too close. This causes intimidation aimed towards the professional so eventually the professional backs off.

Sometimes, if the targeted child or adult gets too close with another person, such as an extended family member or person from the community, the borderline parent or spouse feels threatened. The borderline will give this incidental person a difficult time because of the threat they feel. They feel threatened because they perceive their target could be having a close relationship with someone other than them, the borderline. This relationship the borderline sees may be real or perceived. Regardless, it usually becomes so arduous for the targeted person that all these budding relationships either fizzle out or fray and disappear.

Oftentimes, the borderline is hyper-vigilant about watching their target; they fabricate relationships their targets are involved in when in actuality, there is no relationship at all. The borderline will rage uncontrollably against those they should love the most. They degrade them in ways most people would find despicable. For example, trying to sabotage their child's relationship or feeling threatened when a grandchild is born. They work hard to make sure no one will believe their targeted child or spouse. Many children raised by borderline mothers may have undiagnosed characteristics of attachment disorders in varying degrees.

It is because of the special relationships I have had in my life that I was able to survive life with a Stage Four Borderline and turn into a thriving teen, adult, and parent.

As you read this story, you will gain insight into the varied professionals that saved me. The role of a grandparent is priceless. The impact of both of my grandmothers still resonates with me today. From observing my Grandma Jenny's inner strength to my Grandma Molly's displays of kindness and the art of being genuine, I was able to move forward with tools not available to me in my own home.

My father did not speak for over twenty years, except to answer a question with a yes or no response. There were times he would not speak at all exhibiting selective mutism. My father retreated inward while living with a Stage 4 Borderline. When I left home, he became her new target. For twenty years, I thought I'd never hear his voice again.

It was only upon her death that he started speaking. In the last three years that I had with my father, he gave me two gifts. The first gift was hearing his loving voice once again. The second gift was the opportunity to see my mother through his eyes. It is because of these extra three years with my father that I've been able to understand loyalty and forgiveness. My father loved my mother, even as unbearable as so much of those times were. He lost so much time with his daughter and his many grandchildren and great-grandchildren. But in between the raging episodes with my mother, his wife, he saw her vulnerabilities, her fears, and her desperation. He promised to stand by her and he did, but it cost him dearly. I have learned to make peace with the mother I so much wanted to love but hated. I have spoken to her in death the way I could not speak to her in life. I hope she feels the grace with which I try to see her through the eyes of the man who loved her even in her most unlovable moments.

This is not an easy story to tell. It is easier to keep this door closed. Some have asked me why I would write such a story and reveal this part of my life. That answer is easy. I share my experience in hopes professionals will listen.

Most professionals, from all careers, do not know what borderline personality is and they do not know how to assist a child living in this terror. The cycle of trauma incurred by the children of borderlines can be broken. The cycle of intergenerational trauma caused by familial borderline personality disorder can be broken.

I share my story so more professionals will be able to identify what they are seeing in front of them. With this knowledge, I am hopeful more professionals will view these children through a different set of eyes and reach out to them in a positive way that looks at the whole child, not just as a child with academic or behavior problems.

Sometimes, because of their ignorance of this topic, professionals unintentionally create more stress for the target child. Many professionals have the gift to be able to mold children, to make a difference in their lives. Many carry the futures of these children in their hands. They can provide a nurturing environment where the child can thrive.

Children need to feel safe both at home and at school. When a child does not feel safe at home or at school, that is the recipe for a life that will involve chronic and complex trauma, substance abuse, and involvement with the criminal justice system.

I was one of the fortunate children. I had caring people to stand by me as I navigated the journey of leaving the home of a Stage Four Borderline Mother and broke the cycle. This is my story.

Characteristics of a Borderline Personality Disorder

(According to the DSM-IV-TR, Diagnostic and Statistical Manual for Mental Health Disorders, Fourth Edition, Text Revision)

* Patterns of intense and stormy relationships with family, friends, and loved ones, with extreme idealization (extreme closeness and love) to devaluation (extreme dislike or anger).
* Extreme reactions to abandonment, whether they are real or perceived (panic, depression, rage or frantic actions).
* Distorted and unstable self-image or sense of self, which can result in sudden changes in feelings, opinions, values, or plans & goals for the future.
* Impulsive and often dangerous behaviors, such as spending sprees, unsafe sex, substance abuse, reckless driving, binge eating, and other high risk behaviors.
* Recurring suicidal behaviors or threats of self- harm.
* Intense and highly changeable moods, with each episode lasting from a few hours to a few days.
* Chronic feelings of emptiness and/ or boredom
* Inappropriate, intense anger
* Problems controlling anger

According to the DSM-IV, a person must have shown at least five of the Characteristics above to be diagnosed with borderline personality disorder.

This diagnosis is no longer included in the new DSM -V. At present, there are no medications approved by the U.S. Food & Drug Administration to treat borderline personality disorder.

How I Broke the Cycles of Trauma

* I left home young and emancipated. This is more difficult to do now than it was when I was 16 years old.
* I learned to trust my gut and gain that confidence within myself which started at about 14 years old.
* I have always enjoyed reading, especially biographies and memoirs, celebrating the lives and achievements of others.
* I became comfortable following my instincts. When a situation or concept felt uncomfortable, I would evaluate why I felt uncomfortable, then I would usually do the opposite of the experience I had growing up. Most of the time it worked, sometimes it didn't.
* I surrounded myself with positive, optimistic, and supportive friends who viewed life and the world around us through a more joyous lens.
* It was important to me to step outside myself and embrace others by volunteering and contributing to my community. For example, I worked with victims of rape and was a presenter for the Center Against Sexual Assault. I worked with clients at Planned Parenthood, coached youth sports, was on the Board of Victims for Justice.
* It was important to me to do something profound to help children to have a better life in some small way. I did that by working with high risk youth in the United States to build a school for orphaned children in Central America.
* I have had two sensational, adorable Aussie pups. I play with them often and take them out in the public frequently. People of all ages get a kick out of them, so this experience is uplifting to all of us. Before these two girls, I always had yellow and black labs.
* I take the time to stand still. I make very sure I have a few moments of quiet time for myself. It is usually doing a few postures of yoga on the floor in order to stay grounded or take a long walk.

- I look at the open doors that come my way. Some I do not walk through, many I do.
- I appreciate really simple beauty and I am very aware and nurtured by nature; mountains, animals, the sky, rivers and oceans. I find nature to be an enormous and continuing step for empowerment. Nature, also provides me the ability to see perspective.
- I don't fill my head with negative self-talk. The glass is half full, not half empty. I work very hard to eat clean. That does not mean I will not have a glass of wine occasionally or a piece of birthday cake. I try to be mindful of what I am putting in my mouth, making sure it is good for my body.
- I watch a lot of comedy or meaningful drama, but I do not watch a movie or television show that is laden with violence.
- I have learned to really see people, not just look at them. Then, I trust what I see.
- Empowerment is always a goal for me and for those around me.
- I come from a family of women who have grit. We present with a 'gentle strength'.
- I make it a point to trust my gut.
- I laugh a lot, especially on the most challenging of days!
- And most important, I love my family and friends.
- If you are resilient, you can overcome any adversity!

What is Borderline Personality Disorder?

Most people and professionals do not know what Borderline Personality Disorder (BPD) is. There are many professionals who will not work with them. It is very difficult for me to find professionals willing to work with the borderlines who are more severe. It is considered to be one of the most difficult personality disorders to treat. One of the reasons it was re-organized in the DSV, due to the stigma that is attached to borderline personality disorder.

Professionals are divided as to whether borderlines are aware of their behaviors as they are inflicting them or unaware. Behaviors of a borderline should not be explained away as they can be psychotic in presentation and extremely frightening. I try to keep in mind this disorder has a component that the individual raging is based partly in fear and trauma. It is the ever fluctuating, intensive moods that are challenging for those who want to love them.

According to the National Institute of Mental Health:

Borderline Personality Disorder (BPD) is characterized by pervasive instability in moods, interpersonal relationships, self-image, and behavior.

While a person with depression or bipolar disorder typically endures the same mood for weeks, a person with BPD may experience intense bouts of anger, depression, and anxiety that may last for only a few hours to a day.

Data from a subsample of participants in a national survey on mental disorders, revealed about 1.6 percent, or over five million adults in the United States have BPD in a given year.

BPD usually begins during adolescence or early adulthood. Some studies suggest that early symptoms of the illness may occur during childhood.

Many people with borderline personality disorder may also have another disorder. That is referred to as co-morbidity. The more common co-morbid disorders for women with borderline personality include depression, anxiety, or eating disorders. The more common co-morbidity for men is substance abuse and anti-social personality disorder.

According to the site: "About BPD.com," borderline personality disorder is more common than people think and is more common than schizophrenia. The exact numbers are difficult as many struggle through life without getting diagnosed.

Photographs

Mother enjoing ice cream on a date with dad

Mother at the beach on a date with Dad

Dad visiting relatives prior to meeting Mother

*Mother and Dad on their honeymoon,
Upstate New York 1954*

Mother as a newlywed in 1954

Mother serving Dad breakfast in their new apartment.

Susan at three months old

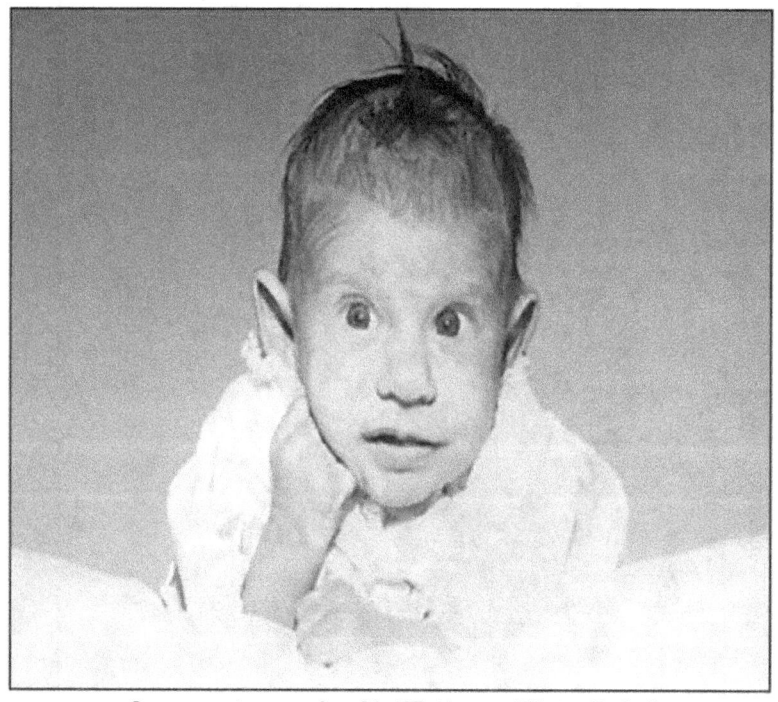

Susan at six months old, "Failure to Thrive Baby"

Susan in Kindergarten

Mother-Daughter portrait 1964
("Mother looks hard and Susan looks haunted")

Dad and Grandma Jenny

Dad grilling Sunday BBQ with family, 1965

Mother hosting Sunday BBQ with family, 1965

Portrait of Mother, 1971

The last photograph of Mother

This last photograph was taken of Dad at the assisted living home a year before he died. He always loved dogs.

About Author

While people are running away from rage and violence, Susan's unique thirty-year career has evolved into one of running into the chaos; identifying and de-escalating rage, creating a circle of safety, and addressing the layers of trauma for those involved. The goal is always to ensure safety and avert tragedy. Susan's consultations with families have included interventions and navigations with parents, youth encompassing the education, medical, legal, and mental health systems. Susan stabilizes rage and anger in high-risk situations with the goal of safety and the trajectory of a positive and productive future for youth and their families. Susan offers expertise in "the other domestic violence" with youth as abuser and parent as victim. It is her number one call out. "Parents believe they are the only family living with nightmare of youth violence in the home. It is more common than many fathom, but it is a secret kept behind the door. Reaching out to me is one of the hardest calls parents makes. It is rewarding and an honor to be part of their positive change."

Susan Magestro is a criminologist and interventionist, international speaker, author, university instructor, teacher, and consultant. Her expertise in the areas of rage and violence have spanned over thirty years, allowing her to develop techniques and strategies that she shares with professionals in the fields of education, counseling, social work, law enforcement and corrections, medicine, mental health, and law. Her work has taken her into schools, medical and mental health facilities, prisons, and into people's homes. The core of her professional experience included working directly with young people and families struggling with rage, trauma, violence, mental health issues, bullying (both cyber and in-person), parental incarceration, and the other domestic violence (youth abuser/parent victim).

Susan has conducted over one hundred classes accredited by the Northwest Accreditation Commission of Colleges and Universities. She has keynoted and lectured internationally and throughout the United States. Susan works with adults and young people on some of the worst days of their lives.

www.ingramcontent.com/pod-product-compliance
Lightning Source LLC
Chambersburg PA
CBHW052143070526
44585CB00017B/1954